Cooking for Silver Foxes
AND OTHER FIRST TIME COOKS

T0265674

ASHLING CLAIRE REVÉ

TATE PUBLISHING
AND ENTERPRISES, LLC

Published by Tate Publishing & Enterprises, LLC
127 E. Trade Center Terrace | Mustang, Oklahoma 73064 USA
1.888.361.9473 | www.tatepublishing.com

Tate Publishing is committed to excellence in the publishing industry. The company reflects the philosophy established by the founders, based on Psalm 68:11,
"The Lord gave the word and great was the company of those who published it."

Book design copyright © 2014 by Tate Publishing, LLC. All rights reserved.
Cover design by Junriel Boquecosa
Interior design by Caypeeline Casas
Photographer: Tonya Visconti
Food Stylist: Chef Jaymes Khademi

Published in the United States of America

ISBN: 978-1-62854-969-0
1. Self-Help / Personal Growth / General
2. Cooking / Health & Healing / Weight Control
14.05.15

DEDICATION

For all the hungry mouths I have
joyfully fed over the years.

THANKS & GRATITUDE

My heartfelt thanks and gratitude to:

Dick Kolar, my favorite "Silver Fox", for inspiring me to write this great little book.

Tonya Visconti, my photographer, for her beautiful work and commitment to the project. You will drool over the results.

My talented chef, Jaymes Khademi, for his valuable input, amazing cooking and wonderful food styling abilities.

My friend CW for never hesitating to get my back; you are 1 in a million.

My friend Tony for encouraging me to think bigger than I ever dreamed.

My friend Cherea for her belief in me.

My friends and family for all their help and support especially those who *showed up* hungry on cook days bringing bottles of wine and willing spirits, and who also helped wash the dishes (you know who you are xoxo), Lolita Kolar, Rob and Elise Wilson, Valerie James, Jerry Heikens, Chef Paul Moir and his wife Laura, Jayson Khademi cook extraordinaire and his beautiful D'Lisa Shayne, John Luke Grubb and his hungry buddies, Alma and Alyssa Arce, Diana Andree, Cherie Jones, Debbie Shields, Carmen and Mario Marsili.

My sisters, Colleen Jacob and Teresa Tagas, for their constant support and encouragement to keep going during the rough times.

John Grubb, who firmly and lovingly pushed me to the finish line.

A special thank you goes to Carmen Marsili for her excellent editing skills which helped this book cross the finish line. Carmen Thanks a million!

A huge thank you to Tate Publishing for recognizing my project and believing in my vision for "Silver Foxes".

FOREWORD BY: DICK KOLAR

When I agreed to work with Ashling for 6 weeks I knew her program would entail several different aspects of health and exercise. However, I didn't know that she would explain the *reasons* for and *benefits* of my exercises. She made me *think* about why I was doing it.

I've always liked walking and exercise and I used to hike a lot on my ranch in Colorado. The first day Ashling took me out to walk she showed me some simple stretching exercises then down the street we went. Even though I was practically falling over by the time I got back to my doorstep, excited, I got in my car and drove the distance to measure how far I had gone. I felt a wonderful sense of accomplishment to have walked 1/6th of a mile. In fact I felt so great I was determined to show Ashling my commitment to her program. The next day it took me over an hour and 15 minutes to walk that first mile long walk, but I did it with Ashling walking backwards in front of me, laughing and encouraging me all the way! She made it fun and it sure beat the hell out of any football practice I ever went to. I gained confidence with each day as well as strength and endurance. My body started to change and my waistline began to shrink. Knowing I was on the right track I decided to really pour it on with the program.

I really looked forward to the social aspects of walking through the neighborhood, meeting my neighbors and making new friends. God gave me this inner self that makes me comfortable being in a crowd and this was no exception. I felt more alive. More like getting out again and doing things. My former depression melted away and I felt a surge of energy and excitement I didn't have before Ashling showed up. I began to play to the crowd again "Eyes open". A sense of happiness and purpose grew in me.

What happened in the kitchen was totally unexpected. I wasn't into cooking and found it interesting but doubted I could duplicate it. However, Ashling won me over by showing me how make healthy food easily, and it certainly tasted a lot better than the food I had become accustomed to. Obviously, food that's healthy and inviting has an impact. Once again I embraced Ashling's attitude and outlook about "thinking" about what I was doing and the benefits I would derive. I began to have an interest where I *never* thought I would go. Sometimes I'm surprised and rewarded by my experimental escapades in the kitchen. Cooking is still a mystery to me at times but I no longer take it for granted. I also see the artistry involved in making food attractive and the opportunity for fulfillment. These very personal achievements have created everlasting benefits in my life. I strongly recommend Ashling's book as a path of achievement and self-esteem, and delicious more healthy food.

In closing, a note to the Author, I want to thank you Ashling for giving me the opportunity to experience a new way of living. You have been the true expression of friendship and caring. You succeeded in opening the door to a new chapter of my life.

Dick Kolar

INTRODUCTION

"Cooking for Silver Foxes... and other first time cooks"

"Cooking for Silver Foxes…and other first time cooks" was inspired by my good friend Dick Kolar. At the tender old age of 83 Dick knew he needed to make a change in his lifestyle. He was living alone and fending for himself for the first time in his life. He'd gained a great deal of extra pounds, had high blood pressure and a heart condition. He felt depressed and lonely and was eating out of bags, boxes and cans. His doctors had given him just a couple of years to live and he was about 1½ years into their prediction. Dick called me asking for help.

As a health coach I understand the benefits and importance of living a healthy lifestyle. I agreed to take 6 weeks from my regular schedule to help Dick accomplish his goals. I packed my bag and headed to Flagstaff to create a personal lifestyle program for Dick. With permission from his doctor for him to take supplements and engage in moderate exercise, we began our epic makeover. Of course I don't recommend waiting until the last hour to make a lifestyle change. It's much easier to start now!

…About four weeks into the program Dick began pulling trousers and sports jackets out of the back of his closet that he hadn't seen in fifteen years. He had great fun trying on his "new" old clothes and was thrilled they fit him again. His pants were so loose they bunched up at the waist when he buckled his belt. Not a very cute look but a sort of "Trophy" in a weird way. He wanted to celebrate by going out to dinner at his favorite restaurant, Josephine's, to show off his new look.

Off we went to see Tony the barber and get Dick all spiffed up with a good haircut and all the important hairs trimmed; next, a much needed manicure. His smile was back and Dick began to see possibilities for the future.

Later when Dick came down the stairs to leave for dinner, you would have thought he was on his way to the prom. He wore a pair of khaki colored wool slacks and a navy blue sports jacket over a red silk shirt; a little red scarf accented his breast pocket. Dick strutted in the front door of Josephine's proud as a peacock. He sang the old standards to all the girls that night and never stopped smiling.

When it came time for me to leave after six weeks, Dick worried that he may not be able to keep up with all the work we had done. I assured him he had everything he needed for continued success with his plan. I gave him a big hug goodbye and expressed how proud I was of his accomplishments and his commitment to the program. He was extremely happy about the tremendous changes he'd made in his lifestyle. Once in a while Dick will call to ask my help in cooking a new dish or to share his latest concoctions. We laugh at his disasters. Hey, we all have them. It's all about the value of eating real food and sharing with others. It's okay to play with your food. Like Emeril Lagasse says "kick it up a notch." Be imaginative and have fun!

Dick lives a healthier, happier, more satisfying life now that he takes responsibility for his health and well-being. Not only that, he feels great. And since his lovely wife Lolita has recovered from an injury and returned home, he loves to dress up and take her out for lunch or dinner now and then.

After settling back into my regular routine, I paged through all the recipes I had written down for Dick. That is when *Cooking for Silver Foxes…and other first time cooks* began to take shape. Here within these pages are the results. Not a diet cookbook, but a path to better choices, more delicious natural foods and a healthier more satisfying lifestyle. Even though some of these ingredients may be new to you, the recipes are simple and easy.

In the back of this book you will find details about the "6 Part Lifestyle Change Program" that helped Dick to make easy, simple, yet profound changes in his lifestyle in just 6 short weeks…

Eat Real Be Well, Ashling Claire Reve

TABLE OF CONTENTS

Breakfast

APPETIZERS

SALADS

DRESSINGS & FLAVORS

SIDE DISHES

ENTRÉES

DESSERTS

Cooking for Silver Foxes and
Other First Time Cooks

BREAKFAST

Blueberry Pancakes
Breakfast Smoothie
Fresh Fruit & Yogurt Parfait
Poached Eggs
Soft Boiled Eggs
Hard Boiled Eggs
Easy Scrambled Eggs
French Chive & Goat Cheese Omelet
Sunday Morning Bacon, Eggs & Spinach Salad
Polenta Cakes w/ Maple Syrup
French Toast w/ Pan Sautéed Apples
Breakfast Potatoes

BLUEBERRY PANCAKES

1 tsp. salt
1½ teaspoons baking powder
2 cups flour
1¼ cups almond milk
1/2 cup plus 1 tsp. vegetable oil
2 large eggs
1 Tbs. sugar
1 Tbs. vanilla extract (optional)
Butter
1 pint fresh blueberries

Whisk together the flour, salt, and baking powder in a medium bowl until well combined. Set aside. Whisk together milk, ½ cup of the oil, eggs, sugar, and vanilla (if using) in a separate large bowl until the eggs are foamy and sugar is dissolved. Add the flour mixture to the liquid mixture and stir until dry ingredients are mixed and moistened (the batter will be lumpy). The batter can sit for up to 12 hours in the refrigerator. Ok, if you want to cheat, get a good quality pancake mix at the health food store and make your batter according to directions. Next, preheat a large non-stick frying pan or griddle to medium/ medium high. The pan is ready when a couple of drops of water dropped in the pan sizzle and pop. Coat the pan with a teaspoon of oil using a paper towel to distribute it evenly. If the surface starts to smoke you need to turn down the heat a little. I usually end up turning the heat down to medium or medium low. Use a measuring cup to ladle ¼ cup of the batter into the pan. Sprinkle blueberries over the tops of the pancakes. Cook until bubbles form over the tops of the pancakes and bottoms are nicely browned, about 2 to 3 minutes. Flip and cook until golden brown on the other side for just about two minutes more. Serve while hot with butter and warm maple syrup. Serves 4

BREAKFAST SMOOTHIE

For each smoothie you will need any combination of *3 or more* of the following fruits:

6 large strawberries frozen or fresh
1 small banana
1/2 cup fresh blueberries
1 orange peeled, seeded and chopped
1 fresh peach or nectarine pitted and chopped
1/2 an apple chopped
1 plum pitted and chopped
4 or 5 dates pitted and chopped
1 cup of almond milk or orange juice
1 fresh egg or 2 egg whites (optional)
2 or 3 ice cubes

Choose *at least 3* of the above fruits for your smoothie. Ripe bananas and dates offer the most sweetness. In a blender cup add fruit, almond milk or juice, fresh egg(s) and ice cubes. Do not pack it too tight. Blend until smooth. Pour into a tall glass and serve with a slice of orange or a strawberry on the side of the rim. Add a piece of toast or a muffin for a satisfying nutritious breakfast. Dick said he could not taste the eggs.

FRESH FRUIT & YOGURT PARFAIT

1 large container Organic or high quality vanilla flavored whole yogurt
1 cup blackberries or blueberries washed and drained
1 cup raspberries
2 bananas sliced
1 cup strawberries washed well and sliced in half
1 cup red seedless grapes
½ cup granola cereal
4 goblets or glass serving bowls

To assemble the parfaits, add about ½ cup yogurt to each bowl. Sprinkle about 2 Tbs. of granola over the yogurt. Next add about ½ cup mixed fruit and berries to each bowl, then add another ½ cup of yogurt over the fruit. Finally, top the yogurt with the remaining granola the rest of the fruit. Use any combination of your favorite fruits and berries.

Sunshine in a bowl, that's what it is! Serves 4

POACHED EGGS

2 eggs
Small parsley sprig
Small shallow fry pan
½ tsp. vinegar

Fill a small shallow frying pan with 2 inches of water and bring to a rolling boil. Line a plate or shallow dish with a folded paper towel. Turn the heat down to very low. Add vinegar to water. Carefully crack the eggs and gently drop into the hot water. Turn the heat up until the water gently simmers. Cook for 3 to 4 minutes until egg whites are opaque and yolks are still soft in the center. Use a slotted spoon to remove them to paper towels to drain excess water. Transfer to a plate or small serving bowl.

Top with chopped parsley and serve with whole grain toast and breakfast potatoes. "Lovely" says Dick!

SOFT BOILED EGGS

Fill a medium saucepan half way with water and bring to a rolling boil. Turn the heat down to low. With tongs add the eggs to the hot water and cover with a lid. Let the eggs cook in the hot water for 7 minutes for a small or medium egg and 8 minutes for large eggs. Use a slotted spoon to transfer the eggs to a medium bowl of cold water until cool enough to handle. Crack the egg gently against the side of the bowl and leave in the water for another minute or so. This helps the shells to peel off easier.

HARD BOILED EGGS

Place eggs in a medium saucepan with a tight fitting lid (the eggs should sit in a single layer). Add enough cold water to cover the eggs by 1 inch. Bring to a boil over high heat, then remove the pan from heat, cover, and let the eggs sit in the hot water for 10 minutes.

Use a slotted spoon to transfer the eggs to a medium bowl of cold water. Gently crack the shells against the side of the bowl and let the eggs sit in the water until cool. Drain and peel.

EASY SCRAMBLED EGGS

"How do you scramble an egg, Ashling??" Dick asked.

2 eggs
2 tsp. butter

Crack whole eggs into a small bowl and lightly blend. Heat a small non-stick frying pan to medium high. Melt the butter until it begins to foam. Pour the eggs into the pan then turn the heat to low. Keeping the heat low when you are scrambling eggs is the secret. Let the eggs sit undisturbed until they begin to set around the edges about a minute or so. Using a wooden spoon or rubber spatula slowly and gently "scrape" the bottom of the pan moving the cooked eggs away from the sides and allowing the uncooked eggs to flow to the bottom of the pan. Do this several times until all the eggs are firm. This takes about 5 minutes. Do not overcook as this will make the eggs tough. With a little practice you will have the most lovely, moist, fluffy scrambled eggs for your breakfast. My granddaughters ask for these eggs whenever they spend the night. Secret….they even ask me to make them for dinner which is easy for me when I'm babysitting.

FRENCH CHIVE OMELET

4 large eggs
1/4 cup chopped fresh chives or scallions
4 oz. goat cheese, cream cheese, or feta
    cheese crumbles
2 Tbs. butter
Salt and fresh ground pepper

Beat eggs well in a small bowl. Chop chives and set aside. Crumble cheese and set aside. Heat your large non-stick frying pan to medium. Melt the butter in the pan until it is foaming and hot. Slowly pour the eggs into the pan and reduce heat to medium low. Cook the omelet slowly allowing the edges to set, about 1or 2 minutes. Tipping the pan slightly, lifting the edges of the omelet occasionally to allow uncooked egg to stream into the bottom of the pan. About 5 minutes total cooking time. When the middle begins to set, sprinkle the chives over the eggs, reserving small amount for the garnish. Then sprinkle the cheese over the eggs. Tip the pan, and lifting the edges of the omelet with your spatula, fold it over in half. Allow the folded beauty to set for a minute then slide the omelet onto a warm plate, top with remaining chives and small amount of cheese and a grinding of fresh black pepper. Cut into portions when serving. Add some toast and orange marmalade, or your favorite Jam. You can serve a small salad of tender greens and some breakfast potatoes with your omelet for a lovely weekend brunch. This is real food!

BREAKFAST SPINACH SALAD W/ POACHED EGGS

8 strips of lean bacon
1 tsp. white vinegar
8 poached eggs (see recipe index)
8 cups fresh spinach
2 large tomatoes cut into 8 wedges each
2 firm avocados
Squeeze of lemon juice
4 very thin slices of red onion
4 oz. goat cheese or feta cheese crumbles
16 pitted Kalamata olives
Red wine vinaigrette (See recipe under "Dressings")
Homemade Croutons (see recipe index)
Salt and fresh ground pepper

First, make your red wine vinaigrette and set aside. Cut bacon strips in half. In a fry pan cook bacon strips on medium low heat until they begin to sizzle. Turn the heat to low and let the bacon cook slowly until browned and crispy. Patience is the key to beautifully crisp bacon. (Cooking bacon slow and low will prevent the fat from spattering all over the stove and also produce nicely browned unburned bacon for your salad). Remove cooked bacon from the pan and drain on a paper towel. Reserve 8 half pieces for topping the salad, and give the rest a rough chop. Set bacon to the side. Peel, seed and cut avocados into slices. Place them on a side plate and sprinkle with lemon juice. In a large salad bowl add spinach, tomatoes (reserve 4 tomato slices for garnishing), red onions, olives and half the cheese crumbles. Place avocados and salad ingredients in the refrigerator to keep chilled until ready to toss.

In a large shallow pan add 2 inches of water and bring to a rolling boil. When very hot reduce the heat to low to stop the bubbling. Add 1 tsp. vinegar to water. Carefully crack eggs into the water one at a time. Turn heat to a very slow simmer. Allow the eggs to simmer on low until the whites are set but still very soft about 3 to 4 minutes. Line a plate with paper towels. Carefully remove the eggs from the water with a slotted spoon and drain on the paper towel. Keep warm.

Toss the chilled salad and avocado slices with the vinaigrette. Divide salad between four plates. Arrange tomato slices on the side. Next gently add the warm poached eggs to the top of the salad. *If the eggs become cold you can rewarm them in a pan of hot, but not boiling hot water for about 30 seconds. Drain them on a paper towel and then add them to the salad. Garnish with the remaining cheese and crispy bacon slices. Finish with a grinding of fresh black pepper. Toasted olive bread is amazing with this outstanding Saturday Brunch Salad. You can even serve this super salad as a great and satisfying summer dinner! Serves 4

FRENCH TOAST W/ PAN SAUTÉED APPLES

6 eggs
1 cup regular or vanilla almond milk
1 tsp. vanilla
1/2 tsp. cinnamon
Pinch of salt
1 Tbs. honey
1 tsp. orange zest
3 Tbs. butter
8 slices of thick white bread (Brioche is my favorite)
2 or 3 red crisp apples, cored and cut into thick slices
Squeeze of lemon juice
1 Tbs. brown sugar
1 tsp. cinnamon
Maple syrup

Sprinkle the apples with lemon juice. In a medium pan melt 2 Tbs. butter with the brown sugar. Add the apple slices and cook on medium for 4 to 5 minutes until apples begin to soften and release their juices and butter and sugar begin to caramelize. Keep your apples warm while you prepare the French toast. Whisk milk, eggs, vanilla, orange zest, salt and honey together in a shallow dish. Heat a non-stick frying pan to medium heat, then add 1 Tbs. butter. Dip bread slices into the eggs coating them evenly on both sides and transfer to the heated pan. The eggs should sizzle just a bit when they touch the pan. Cook the toast until golden brown, flip once and brown the other side, about 6 to 8 minutes in all. Top the French Toast with the warm cinnamon apples and maple syrup.

POLENTA CAKES W/ MAPLE SYRUP

My mother used to serve us polenta, *made from corn grits*, for breakfast with eggs and sausage; a great alternative to potatoes. You can serve it for breakfast, lunch or dinner, sweet or savory. Here we serve it all alone with maple syrup

1 box polenta mix or one refrigerator roll of polenta from the deli section
1 Tbs. butter
Salt and pepper
1/4 cup flour for dusting the polenta slices
1 Tbs. Canola oil
Maple syrup

If using polenta mix, follow directions on package. Pour hot polenta into a buttered glass pan to cool. Polenta will firm up as it cools. When cooled cut into 2 inch squares or slice prepared roll into thick slices. Dust polenta with flour tapping off any excess. Add the oil to a large nonstick frying pan and heat to medium high. When hot, reduce heat to medium. Add polenta slices to your pan and sauté until slightly browned on both sides. Sprinkle with a little salt and pepper to taste.

Serve with warmed Maple syrup.

BREAKFAST POTATOES

8 to 10 medium red potatoes, unpeeled, about 2 to 2 ½ lbs.
1 tsp. salt
2 Tbs. olive oil
1 tsp. fresh rosemary
1 large shallot finely chopped
Good pinch of red chili flakes
Salt and pepper to taste
1/4 cup parmesan cheese *optional
2 Tbs. chopped parsley

Cut potatoes into bite size pieces. In a large pot bring 3 quarts of water and 1 tsp. salt to a rolling boil. Add potatoes and cook until almost done about 6 to 8 minutes. Drain well. Heat your oven to 400'. In a shallow roasting pan toss the potatoes with olive oil, rosemary, shallots, chili flakes and salt and pepper. Roast for 20 to 25 min. until beginning to brown. Stir potatoes and roast for 5 to 10 more min. until nicely browned. Sprinkle with chopped parsley and parmesan cheese. Serve them hot! Omit the rosemary and add chopped red or green peppers for a change in flavors.

APPETIZERS

Salmon Cakes w/ Lemon Honey Vinaigrette
Poached Salmon w/ Dill Sour Cream
Avocado & Yogurt Dip
Guacamole
Hummus w/ Mint & Olive Oil
Marinated Mozzarella Cheese
Hot Deli Olives w/ Parmesan Cheese
Roasted Red Peppers, Garlic & Chiles w/ Crostini
Medjool Dates Stuffed w/ Walnuts & Gorgonzola Cheese
Polenta Marinara w/ Mushrooms
Smoked Salmon Tomato & Red Onion Bruschetta

SALMON CAKES W/ LEMON HONEY VINAIGRETTE

1½ cups poached salmon flaked with a fork
1 scallion thinly sliced
2 Tbs. finely chopped parsley
1 Tbs. Dijon mustard
3 Tbs. mayonnaise
3 cups fresh bread crumbs or Panko bread crumbs
Salt and Pepper
3 Tbs. vegetable oil
4 to 6 cups mixed salad greens

Lemon Honey Vinaigrette

4 Tbs. lemon juice
2 tsp. honey
1 clove garlic smashed
2 Tbs. Dijon mustard
1/2 cup olive oil
1/4 tsp. salt
1/8 tsp. pepper

Combine all ingredients in a jar. Cover tightly and shake vigorously until well combined.

In a large bowl lightly combine the salmon, scallion, and chopped parsley. In a separate bowl combine the mustard and mayonnaise and season with salt & pepper. Add the mayonnaise mixture to the salmon mixture and gently stir together. Add to up to 1 cup of the breadcrumbs to help bind everything together. Shape into 4-6 cakes, depending on desired size, and chill for 1 hour. Lightly press cakes into remaining bread crumbs. Heat oil in non-stick frying pan and cook cakes on each side until golden brown. Serve over mixed greens with Lemon Honey Vinaigrette. You can use crab meat instead of salmon to make great Crab Cakes.

POACHED SALMON W/ DILL SOUR CREAM

1 lb. salmon filet cut into 2 serving portions
2 Tbs. Old Bay seasoning
Enough water to cover the fish plus 1 inch
2 lemons
2 Tbs. finely minced fresh dill or 1 Tbs. dried dill
1/2 cup sour cream

In a large pan, combine Old Bay seasoning, juice of 1/2 a lemon and water. Bring to a boil. Turn down to a slow simmer. Carefully lower salmon filet into simmering water. Cover fish and simmer for 10 to12 minutes until opaque and firm to the touch depending on its thickness. With a large spatula carefully lift the salmon to a paper towel lined plate. When cooled transfer to serving plate and cover loosely with plastic wrap and refrigerate until ready to serve. This can be done a day ahead. Thinly sliced cucumbers and lemon wedges add color and a splash of sunshine!

Dill Sour Cream Sauce: Finely chop fresh dill. Stir dill into sour cream to combine well. Serve with crackers and a bowl of dill sour cream. Poached salmon is great with a crisp green salad and a glass of champagne.

AVOCADO & YOGURT DIP

1 large ripe avocado peeled, pitted, and mashed well
2 cups plain yogurt
Fresh ground black pepper
Squeeze of fresh lemon juice

Mix mashed avocado and yogurt with a fork until smooth. Stir in black pepper and lemon juice. Serve with toasted pita triangles or herbed crackers. Good as a dip for veggies also.

GUACAMOLE

2 ripe avocados peeled, pitted
1 Tbs. lemon juice
Salt and fresh ground pepper to taste
1/2 cup your favorite salsa

Smash avocados in bowl and season with salt and pepper, add lemon juice and salsa. Stir to blend. Chill until ready to serve. Great with tortilla chips, on top of burgers or scrambled eggs, or serve with tacos.

HOT DELI OLIVES W/ PARMESAN CHEESE

Purchase a pint of pitted mixed olives from your grocer's deli. Rinse them well and drain. Place olives in glass serving dish. Drizzle the olives with a teaspoon or so of extra virgin olive oil. Microwave on high for 20 to 25 seconds, depending on how many olives you are warming, sprinkle generously with parmesan cheese and chopped flat leaf parsley. Serve warm w/small spoon or toothpicks. People love these olives warm!

HUMMUS W/ MINT & OLIVE OIL

1 16 oz. can garbanzo beans drained
   and rinsed—some juice reserved
Juice of ½ a lemon
1 garlic clove minced
2 Tbs. olive oil
1/4 cup roasted *Tahini
Salt and pepper to taste
1/4 cup fresh mint leaves coarsely chopped
2 Tbs. pine nuts—optional
Greek pita bread or slices of fresh
   veggies for dipping

Add beans to your small food processor. Add lemon juice, olive oil, garlic, Tahini, salt and pepper and blend until smooth. Add reserved juice or water 1 Tbs. at a time if beans are too thick, until dipping consistency. Check seasonings and adjust if necessary. To serve, spread hummus on a plate, top with pine nuts, and drizzle with olive oil. Scatter fresh mint over the top. Serve with warm pita triangles or sugar snap peas for a delicious healthy snack.

*Tahini is available in most grocery stores.

MARINATED MOZZARELLA CHEESE BALLS

(You can purchase this already marinated, however you can also make your own)

8 oz. container of fresh mozzarella balls, called Boconcini (tiny bite size balls of mozzarella)
1/4 cup extra virgin olive oil
1 tsp. Italian seasoning or 2 tsp. finely chopped fresh herbs of your choice
1/2 tsp. minced fresh garlic
1 Tbs. lemon juice
Dash of dried red chili flakes
Fresh ground pepper
Kosher salt

Drain mozzarella well. In a small glass bowl add herbs, lemon juice, garlic, seasonings, salt and pepper. Whisk well to combine all ingredients. Add mozzarella balls to the bowl and stir gently to coat evenly. Pour olive oil over cheese and gently stir, cover with plastic wrap and chill. Allow to marinate several hours or overnight. Serve with Crostini, recipe below. Before serving taste the cheese and adjust the seasonings if necessary.

Crostini: Slice a baguette in thin slices. Place slices on a cookie sheet and brush with a little olive oil. Toast in the oven at 400' until lightly browned about 5 minutes. You can also use a toaster for this step, and then lightly brush with olive oil after toasting. Sprinkle with parmesan cheese while still warm. Arrange crostini on a warm plate and serve with the marinated mozzarella balls.

ROASTED RED PEPPERS, GARLIC & CHILES W/ TOAST

12 oz. jar roasted red peppers drained and chopped
1 small habanero chili seeded and finely minced (start with ½ a chili, add more
    if you want to kick it up)
1 or 2 cloves of fresh garlic finely minced
Salt and fresh ground pepper
1/4 cup olive oil
1 baguette thinly sliced

While mincing your chili be sure not to touch your eyes or sensitive skin. Wash your hands thoroughly with soap and water afterwards. Stir together all the ingredients, add salt and pepper to taste. Cover and set aside on counter to let the flavors blend.

Slice the baguette and toast lightly on a baking sheet in a 400' degree oven for several minutes. When edges begin to brown remove from the oven and pile toasts into bread basket. Spoon a little of the peppers and oil onto the toast and get ready, there's going to be a party in your mouth. Dick's eyebrows went up when he tasted this hot little dish.

MEDJOOL DATES STUFFED W/ WALNUTS & GORGONZOLA CHEESE

This is one of Dick's favorites!

This recipe can be served as an appetizer or after dinner as a luscious dessert. It is an old time favorite whose popularity has recently reappeared in foodie circles. Medjool dates are larger than the regular ones we are used to seeing in the market. They are also sweeter and softer on the outside than their smaller date cousins therefore making them the most luscious dates on the planet. And I've been told that dates off special "benefits" for all you Silver Foxes!

> 8 large Medjool dates pitted
> 8 walnut halves or approximate in pieces
> 3 Tbs. gorgonzola crumbled

Carefully, with a sharp knife, cut a slit down the side of the date. Remove the pit. Stuff the date halfway with about a teaspoon of the cheese and then stuff in the walnut half or pieces. Arrange on serving plate and chill until ready to serve. Take out about 30 minutes beforehand to serve them at room temperature. These are great with a little glass of Port Wine in the late afternoon; or as a late night dessert in front of the fireplace. They taste amazing warmed in the oven for a few minutes before serving. Serves 4.

POLENTA MARINARA W/ SAUTÉED MUSHROOMS

1/2 lb. mushrooms
2 Tbs. olive oil
1 clove of garlic minced
1/4 cup basil leaves
1 roll of prepared polenta from the deli
section sliced in ½ inch slices
1 jar organic marinara sauce or 1 recipe
of fresh tomato sauce (see recipe index)
1/4 cup parmesan cheese
1/4 cup of white flour for dusting
   the squares of polenta
Salt and pepper

Slice and sauté mushrooms and garlic in 2 Tbs. olive oil. Season with salt and pepper. Remove from heat and set aside. Place the flour in a shallow dish. Coat the polenta slices with a little flour, tapping off the excess. In a large non-stick frying pan heat the olive oil on medium high. Add polenta squares to pan carefully and turn the heat down to medium. Lightly brown the polenta about 3 or 4 minutes on each side. Drain on paper towels. Warm the marinara sauce in small sauce pan. Serve polenta topped with Marinara sauce, sautéed mushrooms and a fresh leaf of basil. Sprinkle generously with parmesan cheese. Serves 4

SALMON TOMATO & RED ONION BRUSCHETTA

Bruschetta is an antipasto (appetizer) from Italy whose origin dates back to at least the 15th Century.

> 1 baguette thinly sliced and toasted – 2 slices for each guest
> 1 pkg. 6 to 8 oz. thinly sliced smoked salmon cut into 16 small pieces

Topping

> 4 ripe tomatoes seeded and chopped
> 1/4 cup finely chopped red onion
> 1/4 cup finely chopped Italian parsley
> 1 clove of garlic finely minced
> 1 or 2 whole cloves of garlic peeled
> 1 Tbs. capers
> 2 Tbs. extra virgin olive oil
> Squeeze of lemon juice
> Salt and fresh ground pepper

For the topping, remove the seeds from the tomatoes and chop coarsely. Toss the tomatoes with the rest of the ingredients. Taste to be sure it is seasoned to your liking. Cover with plastic and chill in the refrigerator until ready to serve. Slice your baguette in thin slices and lay in single layer on a cookie sheet. Place in the oven at 400'. Toast to a light golden brown. Remove from the oven and lightly rub or scrape the top of each slice with the raw garlic clove. This will impart a heavenly garlic flavor to the bread. When you are ready to serve your Bruschetta, arrange the bread slices on a serving platter. Mound a spoonful of tomatoes and onions on top of the bruschetta. Then place a slice of smoked salmon on top of the tomatoes. Top with a little chopped parsley and a few capers. Serve 8.

SALADS

Seared Scallops with Sweet Champagne Vinaigrette
Caprese Salad
Coleslaw w/ Apples, Walnuts & Cranberries
"The Wedge" w/ Red Wine Vinaigrette & Blue Cheese Crumbles
Spinach Salad w/ Lemon Garlic Dressing
Yogurt, Cucumber & Mint Salad
Fruit Salad
Watermelon Slices w/ Red Onions, Feta Cheese & Black Pepper

SEARED SCALLOPS W/ SWEET CHAMPAGNE VINAIGRETTE

10 to 12 cups of organic greens
12 to 16 large scallops
Salt and pepper
1/2 teaspoon of sugar
2 Tbs. butter
2 pink grapefruits
2 small firm avocados
1/2 cup walnut halves
4 oz. goat cheese crumbles
4 very thin slices of red onion
1 Sweet Champagne Vinaigrette (see Dressings and Flavors)

Make the vinaigrette and chill until ready to use. Cut the avocados in half and remove the pit. Carefully slice the avocado into 1/4 inch slices, being careful not to cut through the skin. Using a large spoon scoop the avocado out of the shell and place on a small plate. Drizzle with a little bit of lemon juice to keep avocados from turning brown. Cover loosely with plastic wrap and refrigerate.

Cut the grapefruits in half. Using a small sharp knife section the grapefruit. Remove the fruit with a spoon reserving the juices and fruit and place in a small bowl. Set in the refrigerator to chill.

Ah…now we are ready to sear the succulent scallops. Wash the scallops with cool water and pat them dry with paper towels. Season the scallops with salt and pepper and sprinkle with a pinch of sugar. In a large fry pan on medium high heat melt butter until bubbling. Add half the scallops and sear on both sides 2 to 3 minutes turning them as they begin to brown. They are cooked when they become opaque and firm to the touch. Do not overcook as they will become rubbery. Keep the scallops warm while you cook the remaining half. Add a little more butter if necessary to finish second batch. Meanwhile, add the greens, half of the avocado slices, grapefruit sections and juices, nuts, and half the goat cheese to a large salad bowl. Toss salad with the champagne vinaigrette. Mound the salad on 4 salad plates. Arrange the remaining avocado slices, some reserved grapefruit sections and the warm scallops around the plate. Top with nuts and cheese and serve immediately. Serves 4

CAPRESE SALAD

8 oz. fresh mozzarella (you can use the small Boconcini instead of slices)
3 small ripe tomatoes sliced 1/4 inch thick
1 small bunch of fresh basil leaves
Extra virgin olive oil
Balsamic vinegar
Salt and freshly ground pepper

On a serving plate arrange mozzarella and tomato slices in a circle. Top with thinly sliced fresh basil leaves. Lightly drizzle olive oil and vinegar over the tomatoes and cheese. Season the tomatoes with salt and freshly ground black pepper. Serves 4 to 8.

COLESLAW W/ APPLES, WALNUTS & CRANBERRIES

1 small head of cabbage thinly sliced or 1 16 oz. bag of coleslaw mix
1 ½ cup dried cranberries
1/2 cup celery thinly sliced
1/2 cup chopped walnuts
1/2 cup green onions thinly sliced

Dressing:

1 tsp. of orange zest
3/4 cup mayonnaise
2 Tbs. orange juice
1 Tbs. Honey
1 Tbs. Dijon mustard
Freshly ground black pepper
Salt as needed

Combine cabbage, cranberries, celery, nuts and green onions in a large bowl.

Combine all ingredients for the dressing and stir well. Check for seasoning. Pour dressing over slaw and mix well. Serve chilled. Serves 6 to 8

"THE WEDGE" W/ RED WINE VINAIGRETTE & BLUE CHEESE CRUMBLES

This is a twist on a classic with less calories but all the great taste.

1 Large firm head of iceberg lettuce
4 oz. blue cheese crumbles
Red Wine Vinaigrette (see Dressings and Flavors")

Wash lettuce and remove any bruised outer leaves. Cut lettuce head in half and rinse in cool water keeping the layers of lettuce together. Turn the lettuce halves upside down to drain. Once the lettuce is drained wrap well in paper towels and put in a plastic bag. Place the bag in the refrigerator to chill. Make the Red Wine Vinaigrette adding half the blue cheese. Combine well. When ready to serve the salad remove the chilled lettuce from the refrigerator and cut each half in half again. Now you have 4 wedges. Place each wedge on its back on a chilled salad plate. Pour the dressing over the wedges and top with the remaining blue cheese crumbles and a grinding of fresh black pepper.

Serves 4

SPINACH SALAD W/ LEMON GARLIC DRESSING

10 to 12 cups fresh baby spinach
6 to 8 ounces fresh mushrooms sliced thick
1/4 cup very thinly sliced red onion
1/2 cup pecan pieces
4 oz. crumbled goat cheese
  (you can substitute feta cheese)
4 oz. Pecorino Romano cheese

Juice of ½ a lemon
1/2 tsp. of lemon zest
1/4 cup extra virgin olive oil
Salt and fresh ground pepper
2 cloves of garlic finely minced
Baguette of crusty artisan bread

Mash the minced garlic with the back of a spoon to release the garlic juices. In a small bowl combine the minced garlic, lemon zest and olive oil and set to the side to develop the garlic flavor. In a very large salad bowl add the spinach, mushrooms, red onion, pecans and goat cheese. Cover the salad and chill until you are ready to serve. Add the lemon juice to the olive oil and stir with a small whisk so that it is well mixed. Season the dressing with salt and freshly ground black pepper. Pour the dressing over the spinach salad and toss well.

Mound salad on plates and garnish with some more chopped walnuts and a grinding of fresh ground pepper. With a vegetable peeler shave strips from the side of the Pecorino Romano cheese. Add strips of cheese to the top of the salad. Slices of crusty bread on the side are perfect with this wonderful lemony garlicky salad. This salad mounded on top of warm Chicken Paillards (see Entrees for recipe) is an amazing meal. "Eat it with the one you love" says Dick. Serves 4

*Cooking 101…cook with a friend for unexpected little pleasures. Also good for the heart!

This next recipe is also an amazing way to enjoy your healthy new lifestyle! I know it looks complicated, but go ahead, live on the wild side. Two friends in the kitchen can create not only lovely chemistry and a fabulous culinary treat, but a wonderful experience with truly gratifying results.

YOGURT CUCUMBER SALAD

2 cups of plain yogurt
1 large cucumber
1/4 cup raisins
2 Tbs. fresh mint finely minced

1/4 cup finely chopped walnuts
1/4 tsp. black pepper
4 to 6 Greek pitas breads

Peel and cut the cucumber in half and scoop out the seeds from the inside with a spoon. Grate the cucumber into a medium bowl. Add the rest of the ingredients and stir well. Chill until ready to serve. Cut pita bread into triangles and toast lightly in the toaster if desired.

FRUIT SALAD

2 crisp apples
2 bananas
2 oranges
2 kiwi fruits
4 cups of strawberries
2 cups blackberries

1/2 cantaloupe or other ripe melon
2 Tbs. honey
2 cups vanilla flavored yogurt
Juice of 2 limes
Fresh mint leaves to garnish salad

Combine yogurt, honey and lime juice and mix well. Cover and chill in refrigerator until ready to use. Cut apples in half, remove the core, and cut into bite size pieces. Peel bananas and cut into chunks. Peel oranges, remove any white pith (skin) and seeds and cut into chunks. Peel the kiwi and cut into bite size pieces. Wash strawberries and blackberries thoroughly. Cut strawberries in half, leave the blackberries whole. Peel the rind from the cantaloupe and cut into bite size pieces. Put all the fruit into a large bowl. Pour half the yogurt dressing over the fruit and mix gently to coat the fruit. Serve in bowls with more dressing on the side. Serves 6 to 8

One of the most surprisingly refreshing salads I have ever had. Be brave and give it a try.

WATERMELON SLICES W/ RED ONIONS, KALAMATA OLIVES & FETA CHEESE

1 medium seedless watermelon
1/4 cup red onion very thinly sliced
1/4 cup feta cheese crumbles
1/2 cup pitted Kalamata olives drained
1/2 cup rough slice fresh mint leaves
2 Tbs. high quality white Balsamic vinegar
2 to 3 Tbs. extra virgin olive oil
Pinch of salt
Freshly cracked ground pepper

Wash watermelon well and dry with paper towels. First cut watermelon in half and then in quarters. Then slice the quarters across into ½ inch slices. Arrange melon slices attractively on a large platter. Scatter onions, feta cheese and mint over the top of melon tucking onion slices and mint leaves in between the slices. Lightly drizzle the white balsamic vinegar and then olive oil over the top of the melon slices. Finish salad with a generous pinch of kosher salt and fresh ground black pepper. Serves 8

DRESSINGS & FLAVORS

Oil & Vinegar
Red Wine Vinaigrette
Balsamic Vinaigrette
Sweet Champagne Vinaigrette
Lemon, Garlic & Olive Oil
Yogurt & Avocado Dressing
Honey Lime Dressing
Homemade Mayonnaise
Dill Mayonnaise
Curry Mayonnaise
Spicy Truffle Catsup
Herbs De Provence

OIL & VINEGAR

Sprinkle your salad with salt and pepper. Toss with a teaspoon or so of your favorite vinegar. Use lemon juice instead of vinegar for a refreshing lemon taste. Drizzle the salad with a little extra virgin olive oil and toss again.

RED WINE VINAIGRETTE

1 Tbs. Dijon mustard
1 Tbs. red wine vinegar
2 tsp. finely minced shallots
1/2 tsp. finely minced garlic
1/4 cup olive oil
1/4 tsp. pepper
1/4 tsp. salt

Whisk together the mustard, vinegar, shallots and garlic in a small bowl until very well combined. Slowly drizzle the olive oil into the bowl while whisking constantly. Season the dressing with the salt and pepper.

BALSAMIC VINAIGRETTE

2 Tbs. Balsamic vinegar
6 Tbs. olive oil
1 tsp. brown sugar
1 tsp. finely minced garlic
1/4 teaspoon salt
1/4 teaspoon black pepper

Place all the ingredients in a jar with a tight fitting lid. Shake vigorously until sugar and salt are dissolved. Taste and adjust seasonings. For a lovely variation add 2 tsp. of strawberry jam instead of the brown sugar. This is great on fruit salads.

SWEET CHAMPAGNE VINAIGRETTE

4 Tbs. champagne vinegar
2 Tbs. lemon juice
1 tsp. fine sugar
1/4 tsp. salt
1/8 tsp. black pepper
3/4 cup vegetable oil

In a small blender add the vinegar, lemon juice, sugar, salt and pepper. Pulse several times to combine. Then add the oil and blend well. Adjust the seasonings if needed.

LEMON GARLIC VINAIGRETTE

1/2 tsp. of lemon zest
1/4 cup extra virgin olive oil
2 Tbs. lemon juice
Salt and fresh ground pepper
4 cloves of garlic finely minced
1 Baguette of crusty artisan bread

Mash the minced garlic with the back of a spoon to release the garlic juices. In a small bowl combine the minced garlic, lemon zest and olive oil, season with salt and pepper. This is amazingly garlicky but oh so good for the heart. Be sure you serve this to your partner too because garlic *loves* garlic.

YOGURT & AVOCADO DRESSING

1 cup of plain yogurt
1 avocado
Squeeze of lemon juice
Salt and pepper as needed
2 to 3 Tbs. plain almond milk or regular milk

Peel and remove the pit from the avocado and mash well with a fork.

Add mashed avocado, yogurt, almond milk, and lemon juice to a small bowl and blend until smooth. Season the dressing with salt and pepper. Cover the dressing and refrigerate until ready to use.

HONEY LIME DRESSING

    2 cups vanilla flavored yogurt
    2 Tbs. honey
    Juice and zest of 2 limes

Combine yogurt, honey and lime juice and zest, mix well. Cover and chill in refrigerator until ready to use. This is great over fruit salad or as a dip with a plateful of fresh strawberries.

HOMEMADE MAYONNAISE

    2 egg yolks
    2 Tbs. mustard
    Dash of salt and pepper
    1/2 tsp. of lemon juice
    1 to 1½ cups vegetable oil

Add the yolks, mustard, lemon juice, salt and pepper into a small blender on low. Slowly add 1 cup of the oil until you have the desired consistency. Add more if necessary.

DILL MAYONNAISE

1/2 cup mayonnaise
1 Tbs. fresh dill finely minced

Mix fresh dill and mayonnaise together well. Cover and refrigerate several hours to let dill flavor develop. Serve with poached salmon and crackers.

CURRY MAYONNAISE

1/2 cup mayonnaise
1 tsp. curry powder

Mix curry powder and mayonnaise together well. Cover and refrigerate several hours to let curry flavor develop. Serve as a dipping sauce for cold shrimp or poached salmon. It's also great on grilled chicken or asparagus spears or as a dip for veggies.

SPICY TRUFFLE KETCHUP

    1 cup catsup
    1 tsp. hot sauce
    2 tsp. black truffle oil

Combine all ingredients in a small bowl and refrigerate until ready to use.

HERBS DE PROVENCE

This classic herb blend calls for dried herbs.

    3 Tbs. dried tarragon leaves
    1½ Tbs. dried savory leaves
    1 Tbs. dried sage leaves
    1 Tbs. dried thyme leaves
    1 Tbs. dried lavender buds
    1 Tbs. dried marjoram leaves

In a bowl stir herbs together until well combined. Store them in a container with a tight fitting lid.

SIDE DISHES

Lemon Green Beans w/ Toasted Almonds
Asparagus
Baked Potatoes w/ Veggies & Parmesan
Mashed Potatoes
Dicki's "Smashed" Potatoes
Roasted Fingerling Potatoes
Mexican "Street" Corn on the Cob
White or Brown Rice in the Rice Cooker
Quinoa w/ Crispy Pancetta
Roasted Garlic

LEMON GREEN BEANS W/ TOASTED ALMONDS

1/2 lb. fresh green beans
1 Tbs. butter
1 small shallot finely chopped

2 Tbs. sliced almonds
Salt and pepper to taste
A squeeze of lemon juice

Add a couple inches of water and 1 tsp. of salt to a large shallow pan and bring to a boil. Add green beans and cook until fork tender, about 4 to 6 minutes. Transfer to a colander and drain. In the same pan add butter, shallots and sliced almonds. Cook on medium low heat until almonds are slightly browned. About 1 to 2 minutes. Return green beans to pan and toss with the butter, shallots and almonds. Add salt and pepper to taste and squeeze a little lemon juice on beans and toss lightly once more. Serves 4

ASPARAGUS

1 lb. fresh asparagus
1 Tbs. butter
1 tsp. salt for cooking,

Salt and pepper to taste
Squeeze of fresh lemon juice

Add a couple inches of water to a large sauté pan and bring to a good simmer. Add 1 tsp. salt. Trim the bottom ¼ off the stems of the asparagus spears. Add the asparagus to the simmering water and cook until tender about 4 to 6 minutes (do not overcook) then rinse well with cold water and drain. When ready to serve melt butter in the sauté pan and return asparagus to pan to warm them and give them a slight glaze of butter. Sprinkle with lemon juice, salt and pepper to taste. Or serve cold asparagus with homemade mayonnaise flavored with curry or lemon and dill. Serves 4

BAKED POTATOES

1 medium russet potato or sweet potato for each person
Vegetable oil to coat the potatoes

Scrub each potato well. Coat them with vegetable oil and wrap in foil. Bake at 350' degrees for 1 hour. For larger potatoes bake an extra 5 min. They are done when a toothpick is inserted easily. Cool potatoes in their foil. Remove the foil before serving. Split potato down the middle and add a *little* butter or a spoonful of plain yogurt. A great healthy suggestion is to top your potato with broccoli florets, sautéed mushrooms or other favorite steamed vegetables and sprinkle with some parmesan or feta cheese crumbles; what a great alternative to all that phony *franken-cheese sauce.*

MASHED POTATOES

2 lbs. potatoes
4 Tbs. butter
1/2 to 3/4 cup plain almond milk or regular milk
2 Tbs. fresh chopped chives
Salt and pepper to taste

Peel and cut potatoes into 1 inch cubes. In a large saucepan add 1 Tbs. of salt and enough water to cover the potatoes by 1 inch. Bring to a boil and cook potatoes until very tender, about 8 to 10 minutes. When done, drain potatoes and allow them to cool for 15 minutes. Transfer potatoes back to the cooking pot. Add butter and milk. With a hand mixer beat on high until smooth. If you want some added flavors you can toss in some roasted garlic. Add more liquid if needed. Add salt and pepper to taste. Re-warm the potatoes on a very low heat stirring often so they don't burn. Top with chopped chives.

DICKI'S "SMASHED" POTATOES & CORN

10 red potatoes washed and quartered
1 small can of corn, rinsed and drained
   or 1 cup fresh corn off the cob
4 to 6 green onions chopped
2 Tbs. butter
1/2 cup of plain unsweetened
   almond milk or regular milk
Salt and pepper to taste
2 cloves of garlic minced

Cook potatoes about 8 to 10 minutes until tender then drain well. Return to cooking pan. Smash potatoes roughly with a potato masher. Add the rest of ingredients to smashed potatoes and fold together. Adjust salt and pepper to your taste. Add more liquid if necessary. You can add chopped bacon or veggies of your choice and any kind of "left overs" you have to these wonderful smashed potatoes. Cut veggies or meats into small bite sized pieces. Really! The variations are endless.

ROASTED FINGERLING POTATOES

2 lbs. fingerling potatoes
Olive oil
Salt and pepper
Pinch of sugar
1/4 cup chopped fresh parsley or other herbs, optional

Line a baking sheet with foil. Heat 3 quarts of water to boiling. Add whole potatoes to water and cook 12 to 15 minutes until tender when pierced with a fork. Drain well. Place cooked potatoes on a baking sheet and toss with olive oil, salt and pepper. With a potato masher lightly mash down potatoes just to break them up a little. This will add delicious crispy brown edges to the potatoes. This would be a great time to sprinkle some fresh chopped herbs over the potatoes for added flavors. Roast potatoes at 400' degrees for 20 to 30 minutes or until nicely browned. Serves 4 to 6

MEXICAN "STREET" CORN ON THE COB

 4 ears of fresh corn
 1 cup parmesan cheese
 1/4 cup of mayonnaise
 1/4 cup parsley finely chopped

In an oblong glass dish mix together the parmesan cheese and parsley until well blended. Remove the outer leaves and the silk from the corn and wash well. On a hot grill roast the corn for 4 to 5 minutes. Turn the corn every minute or so until slightly browned. While ears are hot, use a pastry brush to spread the mayonnaise on the corn. Immediately roll the ears of corn in the parmesan cheese mixture until lightly coated. Pile them up on a big platter and serve 'em hot! This *is* sort of decadent. Moderation is the key! We all went crazy loco for this one!

WHITE OR BROWN RICE

Using your rice cooker is an easy way to cook your grains.

 1 cups white rice, brown rice, or quinoa
 2 cups water
 1 Tbs. olive oil
 1/4 teaspoon salt

Add all ingredients to your rice cooker. Put on the lid. Turn it on. When the rice is cooked it turns itself off! How easy is that? Fluff with a fork. ***If you do not have a rice cooker, "Get one" says Dick! You can always follow the directions on the package of rice. But seriously, let's make this easy. Serves 4

QUINOA W/ CRISPY PANCETTA

1 cup quinoa
2 cups water
1 Tbs. olive oil
1 cup cooked baby peas
   (available in the frozen
   vegetable section)

2 lg. shallots thinly sliced
4 ounces of chopped pan-
   cetta (or bacon)
1 Tbs. butter
Salt and pepper to taste

In a rice cooker add quinoa, water, 1Tbs. of olive oil, 1/2 tsp. salt. Cook until done, or follow directions on package. Chop pancetta in ½ inch pieces. In a small frying pan add about1 tsp. of olive oil and heat to medium. Fry the pancetta and shallots together on a medium until browned and pancetta is slightly crispy. Set aside. Cook the peas according to the directions and drain. Transfer quinoa to a serving bowl, add salt and pepper if needed. Gently fold in peas, butter and 2/3 of the crispy pancetta. Top with remaining pancetta and serve hot. You can add bite size pieces of Chicken or other meat to your quinoa and make this into a one dish meal. Healthy too!

ROASTED GARLIC

1 to 3 heads of fresh garlic
1 Tbs. olive oil
Coarse salt
Foil lined baking dish

Set the oven at 375'. Remove the dry outer layers of skin from the garlic heads leaving them whole. With a sharp knife slice approx. 1/4 inch off the top of the garlic heads. Place them in the baking dish and toss them with the olive oil and a sprinkling of salt. Bake for 20 minutes until soft and slightly browned. Place warm garlic heads in a clean jar with a tight fitting lid. Fill the jar with enough olive oil to cover the roasted garlic. Store the jar in a cool place. Good for about 2 to 3 weeks. The serendipity here is that as the garlic sits in the oil it gives the oil a wonderful garlic flavor and you can use the roasted garlic cloves as you need them. Great for dipping bread!

ENTRÉES

Fish Tacos
Pan Sautéed Fish w/Capers & Lemon
Baked Fish w/ Herbs
Grilled Salmon
Teriyaki Salmon Rice Bowl w/ Broccoli
Salmon Cakes w/ Honey Lemon Vinaigrette
Roasted Whole Chicken w/ Herbs de Provence
Baked Chicken Breast & Pieces
Chicken Cutlets
Warm Chicken Paillard Topped w/ Lemony Garlic Spinach Salad
Chicken Kabobs w/ Basmati Rice
Dick's Big Blue Bacon Turkey Burger
Turkey Meat Loaf
Turkey Meat Balls
Pork Loin Roast
Pork Loin Lettuce Wraps
Filet Mignon w/ Warm Goat Cheese & Balsamic Reduction

FISH TACOS

1 to 1½ lbs. fish filets such as Red
    Snapper or Cod
(You can also make these tacos
    with Shrimp too!)
2 eggs beaten
Fine bread crumbs
Canola oil
Salt and pepper to taste
8 limes

1/2 cup mayonnaise
1 lg. ripe avocado
2 to 3 Tbs. milk
1 bottle dark red salsa
1/2 head of green cabbage *thinly* shaved
16 fresh corn tortillas
1 large can refried beans heated
1 cup crumbled Mexican Cotija
    cheese or shredded jack cheese

Green Avocado Sauce: Mash avocado very well with a fork in a small bowl until smooth. Add milk 1 Tbs. at a time until smooth. Season it with salt, pepper and a squeeze of lime.

White Lime Mayonnaise: Add juice of 4 limes to 1/2 cup mayo and combine well. Add salt if necessary.

Red Sauce: Purchase a dark red salsa at the store.

Fill 3 small serving bowls with the sauces. With a sharp knife very finely shave the cabbage. Place on serving plate. Wrap tortillas in foil and place them in the oven at 300' to warm up while you cook the fish.

Wash fish in cool water and pat dry with paper towels. Cut fish into 2 inch by 1 inch strips. Season your fish lightly with salt and pepper. Dip fish pieces in egg and then roll them in bread crumbs pressing slightly so that crumbs adhere to fish. In large frying pan heat oil on medium high then turn down the heat to medium. Don't overcrowd the pan while cooking. Cook fish until golden brown and crispy then transfer to a warm plate lined with paper towels. Drizzle with a little lime juice right before serving. Using 2 tortillas for each taco fill with several pieces of fish and shredded cabbage. Drizzle tacos with a little Lime Mayonnaise Sauce. Serve with refried beans, sauces, and wedges of lime. The Mexican "Street" corn is a great addition to these tacos. Serves 4

PAN SAUTÉED FISH W/ CAPERS & LEMON

2 lbs. of fish filets such as Cod, Red Snapper, Swai or Basa
1/2 cup flour
1 very juicy lemon
3 Tbs. capers
4 Tbs. butter
1 Tbs. canola oil
Salt and pepper to taste

Rinse fish with cool water and pat dry with paper towels. In a shallow dish coat fish lightly with flour and shake off as much excess as possible. Lay fish on a dry plate and set aside. In a large non-stick pan on medium high heat, melt 2 Tbs. butter and 1 Tbs. oil. Add fish and turn heat to medium. Pan sauté filets about 3 minutes on each side to a nice light golden color. Turn carefully with a spatula. Salt and pepper lightly. When done cut the lemon in half and squeeze the juice over the fish and into pan. Immediately add the capers and remaining 2 Tbs. of butter. It should bubble up when it hits the pan. Swirl fish in the lemon juice and capers and the sauce will thicken slightly. Do not overcook. Just a little tip: Swai is a lot more delicate than Cod or Red Snapper. It can fall apart if you handle it roughly, but it still tastes good. Remove fish to the plate and top with pan sauce and a wedge of lemon. Serve immediately. Serves 4

BAKED FISH W/ TOMATOES & "HERBS DE PROVENCE"

2 lbs. fresh fish filets such as Cod,
    Red Snapper, Swai or Basa
1 Tbs. olive oil, canola, or vegetable oil
1 medium can of diced tomatoes
2 Tbs. butter
4 sprigs of parsley

Juice of 1 lemon
1/2 tsp. dried "Herbs de Provence" (see
    recipe index) or herbs of your choice
    such as dill, rosemary, basil or oregano
1/4 cup grated parmesan cheese
1/4 cup bread crumbs Salt and pepper

Wash fish in cool water and pat dry with paper towels. Line up fish filets in glass baking dish. Season the fish well with salt and pepper and herbs. Add the diced tomatoes. Mix together the cheese and bread crumbs and sprinkle over the top. Bake at 350' for 20 to 25 min. until the fish is opaque and firm. Serves 4

GRILLED SALMON

Four 6 oz. salmon filets
Salt and pepper
Cooking spray
2 Tbs. honey

Dijon mustard
1 Tbs. minced shallots
1 Tbs. Lemon juice
1 Tbs. brown sugar

In a small bowl combine honey, mustard, shallots, lemon juice and sugar and set aside.

Make a foil cooking package for the salmon (see photos). Spray foil package with cooking spray or coat with a teaspoon of vegetable oil.

Season salmon filets and place skin side down on foil grilling package. Brush with sauce and grill on medium heat for 10 to 12 minutes depending on the thickness of your fish. It is not necessary to turn the fish over as it is cooking. Fish is done when opaque and firm to the touch. Brush with sauce again when done grilling. Remove from grill and transfer salmon to serving plate. Serves 4

TERIYAKI SALMON & RICE BOWL W/ BROCCOLI

Four 4 to 6 salmon filets
Salt and pepper to taste
1 bottle teriyaki sauce
4 cups broccoli florets
Cooking spray
2 Tbs. chopped cashew nuts (optional)
4 sprigs of cilantro
1 recipe of cooked white or brown rice

Make a foil cooking package for the salmon as shown in the Grilled Salmon recipe. (See photos). Spray foil package with cooking spray or coat with a tsp. of vegetable oil.

Season salmon filets well and place skin side down on foil grilling package. Brush lightly with teriyaki sauce and grill on medium heat for 10 to 12 minutes. It is not necessary to turn the fish over as it cooks. When fish is cooked through, brush once more generously with sauce. Transfer to a plate and keep warm. Remove skins before serving. In a medium sauce pan bring water and 1 tsp. salt to a boil. Add the broccoli and cook for about 3 minutes. Rinse with cold water and drain well. Warm the remaining sauce in a small pan to top off the "Teriyaki Bowls". Serves 4 to 6

Fill bowls with rice, top with broccoli and salmon. Spoon a little more sauce over the top. Sprinkle top with finely chopped cashew nuts and sprigs of cilantro. Serve extra teriyaki sauce on the side. You can make a rice bowl out of just about anything including leftovers and a bottle of well-chosen sauce. Dick says you should read the label and be sure you pick a healthy one.

ROASTED WHOLE CHICKEN W/ HERBS DE PROVENCE

1 whole chicken 3½ to 5 lbs.
Cooking spray
Salt and pepper
1 Tbs. dried Herbs de Provence (see recipe index)
1 Tbs. olive or canola oil

Set oven to 350'. Get a small meat thermometer at the grocery store or kitchen outlet. Line baking sheet with foil and spray with cooking spray. Rinse chicken thoroughly in cold water and dry inside and out with paper towels. Mix salt, pepper and herbs together in a small bowl. Rub the chicken inside and out with the seasonings. Tuck the wings back and place chicken on a rack in a roasting pan. Drizzle the chicken with olive oil. Roast chicken for 65 to 75 minutes or until the internal temperature reaches 170 degrees. With a pastry brush generously baste the chicken with pan juices about every 20 minutes. The results will be a beautiful, succulent, golden bird sure to impress. Remove from the oven, tent loosely with foil and let the chicken rest at least 20 minutes before slicing. Leftovers are great for sandwiches, lettuce wraps, and chicken tacos. Roasting a whole chicken gets easier each time you do it. Get a small meat thermometer at the grocery store or kitchen outlet. Serves 4

BAKED CHICKEN BREAST & PIECES

Cut up chicken pieces
Salt and pepper
Herbs de Provence (see recipe index)

Olive or canola oil
Cooking spray
Preheat the oven to 350'

Line the baking sheet with foil and spray with cooking spray. Season the chicken pieces with salt, pepper and herbs and place on the baking sheet. Drizzle with oil. Bake at 350' for 50 to 60 minutes until done. Leave in oven 10 to 15 minutes longer for bigger pieces of chicken. Brush with pan juices a couple of times during baking. Serves 4

CHICKEN CUTLETS

My kids call it "flat chicken", I call it amazingly good!

4 skinless boneless chicken breasts
Salt and pepper
2 large eggs

2 cups fine bread crumbs
    plain or seasoned
Canola oil

Wash chicken pieces and pat dry with paper towels. Cut each chicken breast into 2 to 3 pieces. Place 2 to 3 pieces in a large Ziploc bag and close pushing out as much air as possible. With a meat pounder/ tenderizer, flatten meat to 1/4 inch thick. Beat eggs in a shallow bowl. Dip pieces of chicken in the beaten eggs and then coat them with bread crumbs. Shake off excess crumbs. Layer the chicken pieces between waxed paper while preparing the rest of the chicken. Heat the canola oil in large frying pan on medium high. Add chicken pieces and turn to medium low heat, slowly frying until golden brown and crisp. Transfer to paper towel lined plate to drain. You can serve this delightful chicken with a side dish and a lovely salad. These chicken wonders are also great cold for a picnic and they make a great sandwich, hot or cold, layered with a little mustard, lettuce and tomatoes. I suggest you make plenty of these tasty chicken bites to ensure leftovers for the next day. Dick always does this! Serves 4 or more

WARM CHICKEN PAILLARD TOPPED W/ SPINACH MUSHROOM SALAD

4 skinless boneless chicken breasts
1 cup of flour in a shallow dish for
    dusting the chicken
Salt and pepper
1 large container fresh baby spinach
2 cups fresh mushrooms sliced
2 Tbs. thinly sliced red onion
2 cloves of garlic squeezed through
    a garlic press

1/4 cup olive oil
2 Tbs. lemon juice
1 tsp. salt
A couple grindings of pepper
1/2 tsp. lemon zest
1/2 cup walnut pieces
Fresh grated parmesan cheese

Add garlic, salt and pepper, the lemon juice and lemon zest to a small jar with a tight fitting lid and shake well. Add 1/4 cup canola oil and shake vigorously to blend well. Set the vinaigrette aside to let the flavors develop.

Wash the chicken pieces and pat dry with paper towels. Cut each chicken breast in half. Place 2 pieces at a time to a large Ziploc and close pushing as much air out as possible. With a meat pounder/tenderizer, flatten chicken meat to 1/4 inch thick. Dust with flour, shaking off excess. Layer the chicken between waxed paper while preparing the rest of the pieces. Set aside. Heat the canola oil to medium high. Carefully lay chicken pieces in hot oil, do not crowd the pan. Turn heat down to medium or medium low. Cook for 2 to 3 minutes on each side until golden brown. Season with salt and pepper. Transfer chicken to paper towel lined plate and keep warm until all pieces are cooked.

In a large salad bowl place enough fresh spinach to serve four people. Add mushrooms, red onion and walnuts and a little salt and pepper. Add enough garlic vinaigrette dressing to lightly dress the salad and toss. Lay 2 pieces of warm chicken on a dinner plate then mound your spinach salad on top of the chicken. Sprinkle with parmesan cheese and top generously with more walnuts and fresh ground pepper. Serve your delicious healthy salad with a slice of crusty bread and oven roasted fingerling potatoes. "A greatly satisfying dinner" Dick said!

CHICKEN KABOBS W/ BASMATI RICE

4 boneless skinless chicken breast halves
1 medium onion grated into a bowl
2 lemons juiced
6 Tbs. butter cut into pieces
8 small plum tomatoes tossed with
   1Tbs olive oil, salt and pepper
2 cups Basmati rice
1/4 tsp. ground saffron
4 Tbs. butter
1 red pepper

2 medium zucchini
Fresh mushrooms, about 12
1 cucumber grated into a separate bowl
2 cups of plain yogurt
1/4 cup walnuts finely chopped
1/4 cup raisins
1/4 cup fresh mint finely chopped
Salt and fresh ground pepper
12 wooden skewers soaked in water

For the kabob, soak the wooden skewers in water while you are preparing the chicken. This is so the wooden skewers won't burn while you are grilling the meat. Add the lemon juice to the grated onion. Cut chicken into 1½ by 1½ inch pieces then add to the onion and lemon. Cover with plastic and refrigerate turning pieces occasionally up to 8 hrs. Skewer the chicken pieces on 8 skewers. Season the kabobs with salt and pepper. Melt 4 tbs. of butter with 1/4 teaspoon of saffron. Brush kabobs several times lightly with the saffron butter during grilling. Grill on medium heat 4 to 5 min on each side depending on size of kabob pieces. Brush again with remaining butter before removing from the grill. Serves 4

For the grilled veggies cut the veggies into bite sized pieces. Make 4 skewers of veggies and grill while cooking chicken, turning to make grill marks on all sides.

Add 2 cups of rice and 4 cups of water to your rice cooker. Add 1/2 tsp. of salt and 2 Tbs. butter. Cook as directed. Fluff rice while still warm with a fork when done.

Cucumber Yogurt (see recipe index)

Serve kabobs on top of white rice. Add grilled veggies and cucumber yogurt on the side.

DICK'S BIG BLUE BACON TURKEY BURGER

"My bacons' got the blue burger blues" (Dick singing). These burgers are not for those shy about chowing down in front of others. They are hefty ½ pounders. Dick says, "Throw yourself into these burgers". You will have no regrets!

2 lbs. ground Turkey
Salt and pepper
4 slices crisp bacon cut in half
4 oz. crumbled blue cheese
1 Red onion sliced thinly
1 large beefsteak tomato cut into 4 thick slices
Green leaf lettuce washed and chilled in the refrigerator
4 large hamburger rolls like Kaisers or similar rolls
Mayonnaise, Dijon mustard, catsup
Cooking spray for the grill

Form the ground turkey into 4 large thick burgers about ¾ inches thick. Season the burgers with salt and lots of fresh ground black pepper. Press the pepper lightly into the burger. Refrigerate on a plate until 5 min before ready to grill.

For each burger prepare a large thick slice of tomato, thin slices of red onion and crisp lettuce leaves. Allow for 1 Tbs. of blue cheese for each burger. Fry bacon slowly on low heat and you will get the nicest crispy bacon ever. Drain on paper towels and set to the side. Split the burger rolls in half if not already sliced.

Are you ready for the grill? Now, preheat your grill to medium high.

Spray the grill well with pan spray being careful not to fan the fire too much. Grill burgers about 5 to 7 minutes on each side for medium. The meat will be firm to the touch when done. Carefully turn turkey burgers when cooking. Ground Turkey is less firm than regular ground beef and they may fall apart if handled roughly. Just before burgers are finished grilling top each burger with 2 pieces of the bacon, and 1 Tbs. of blue cheese crumbles. Lay the burger rolls cut side down on the grill for a few seconds to toast lightly. Dick says *Do not burn the buns!* They must be tender enough to accept the succulent juices from this mouthwatering turkey burger, grilled to perfection, dripping with blue cheese, dressed up with crispy bacon, onions, a juicy slice of Tomato and beautiful green lettuce. Add whatever condiments you like. Dick says: get yourself an ice cold beer to go with this one. No regrets.

Variations: Using the same burger preparation you can change it up by using these different ideas for toppings and flavors: slices of roasted green chilies with jack cheese, top with spicy chili and cheddar cheese, or sliced avocado and slices of apple and caramelized red onions, you get the idea. You can also use ground beef. I suggest grass fed beef or bison, even ostrich! Take a walk on the wild side….says Dick!

TURKEY MEAT LOAF

1½ lb. of ground turkey or beef
1 egg
1/2 cup onions finely chopped
1/2 cup fine breadcrumbs
1/2 cup tomato sauce
1/4 teaspoon anise seeds
1/4 cup grated parmesan cheese
1 Tbs. dried marjoram or oregano
    or basil, or combination
1 clove garlic finely minced
Salt and pepper to taste

In a large mixing bowl combine all ingredients well. Add salt and pepper to taste and mix well. Gently press meat into a loaf pan smoothing the top surface with your hands. Top with a little tomato sauce or a drizzle of catsup, and Bake at 350 degrees for 1 hour and 15 minutes. Test with a toothpick for doneness. If it comes out clean, it's done. It's a lighter and healthier version when you use ground turkey instead of beef. Cool for at least 20 minutes before slicing. Store the remaining meat loaf wrapped in plastic in the refrigerator to make awesome grilled meatloaf sandwiches. Serve it with crusty bread, homemade mayonnaise, catsup, and some pickles. Add some brie cheese or some cold unsalted butter slices for the bread, some grapes or crisp and juicy apples and a nice bottle of wine. Dick thinks picnics are definitely a great way to a "Silver Fox's" heart.

TURKEY MEAT BALLS

Using the same recipe for Meatloaf form your meat mixture into 1 inch balls with your hands and line them up on a foil lined cookie sheet. Bake in the oven for 20 to 30 minutes depending on how big you make them. Cool meatballs and store in a large Ziploc baggie. You can freeze them for future use or add to your spaghetti sauce.

Another easy way to cook your meatballs is right in your lovely bubbling tomato sauce. Form meat mixture into 1 inch balls and add to your bubbling hot tomato sauce. (recipe follows) Once you have added all the meat to the sauce turn it down to very low simmer and cook meat balls without disturbing them for at least 10 minutes. Then gently turn the meatballs with a big spoon to make sure they cook evenly. Taste one of the meatballs for doneness. Yum! Cooking them this way adds richness and flavor to your tomato sauce.

Remember, you can use a variety of meats for this recipe.

To make a great meatball sandwich split a hoagie roll and toast it lightly under the broiler or in the toaster oven. Place 3 to 4 warmed up meatballs on the roll, add a big spoonful of tomato sauce and sprinkle with some grated mozzarella cheese. Place under the broiler for a minute or so to melt the cheeses. A small green salad on the side makes this a great meal.

FRESH HERB ROASTED PORK LOIN

Dick says this is one of his favorites!

    3 lb. pork loin roast
    Salt and pepper to season
    Olive oil
    Salt and pepper
    1 tsp. dried Thyme

Season the roast with salt and pepper and herbs. Heat 1 Tbs. olive oil in an oven proof skillet on medium high. Brown the roast on all sides. Place the skillet in the oven, uncovered, for 30 min at 325'. Brush the meat with pan drippings or grilling sauce in 15 minutes and again when you take it out of the oven. Roast until the internal temperature of the meat reaches 140 degrees. Cool for at least 10 minutes before slicing. Use the leftover roast for tacos and lettuce wraps or make a grilled pork sandwich. Serves 4

PORK LETTUCE WRAPS

4 cups diced roast pork loin or other already
cooked meat such as chicken or beef
One large head of iceberg lettuce
1 small can of water chestnuts drained and chopped
2 green onions thinly sliced
1 bottle of purchased teriyaki sauce or
other any other sauces that turn you on.

To prepare lettuce leaves cut head of lettuce in half from the core down, keeping the layers of lettuce together, rinse thoroughly and turnover on kitchen towels to drain. Wrap lettuce loosely in
paper towels, place in a plastic bag and refrigerate. Warm the diced pork quickly in a large sauté pan
over a medium high heat, about 1 minute. Do not overcook. Add about 1/4 cup of sauce to moisten
the meat. Stir in water chestnuts and green onions. Remove from the heat and transfer meat to a
serving bowl. When you're ready to serve your wraps, carefully separate the lettuce leaves keeping
them as whole as possible. Arrange leaves on a platter with the bowl of meat in the middle. Serve
immediately with extra sauce on the side. Wrap a generous spoonful of meat mixture and spoonful of teriyaki sauce in your lettuce leaf and enjoy. So easy! You substitute chicken instead of Pork.
Allow at least 2 lettuce wraps per person. Serves 4

FILET MIGNON W/ WARM GOAT CHEESE & BALSAMIC REDUCTION

1½ cups of good quality balsamic vinegar
3 Tbs. sugar
2 Tbs. Butter
Four 6 oz. filet mignon steaks
about 1/2 inches thick
Salt and lots of fresh coarse black pepper
4 oz. soft fresh goat cheese

Bring the balsamic vinegar and sugar to a boil in a small saucepan over medium heat. Reduce to a simmer and cook, stirring occasionally for about 15 minutes until very thick and syrupy. Set to the side.

Meanwhile, preheat the broiler. Melt the butter in a heavy large skillet over medium-high heat. Sprinkle the steaks generously with salt and fresh ground pepper. Pan Sauté the steaks to desired doneness, about 5 minutes per side for medium-rare. Transfer the steaks to a foil lined baking sheet. Add 1 oz. goat cheese to top of the steaks and broil just until the cheese begins to melt, about 1 minute. Transfer the meat to serving plates. Drizzle the balsamic sauce around the steaks and add a sprig of parsley. Serve more reduction on the side. Serves 4

DESSERTS

Open-Faced Plum Tart
Fresh Strawberries w/ Balsamic Reduction
Chocolate Sorbet Soda
Berries & Pound Cake w/ Whipped Cream
Fruit & Cheese Plate
Lemon Cake
Chocolate Ganache

OPEN-FACED PLUM TART

Just fresh seasonal fruit, a tiny bit of sugar and you have the makings of a great pie. Oh, you never made one? Here's any easy way to stretch your culinary skills. The rewards are delicious! I saw this easy tart being made on the cooking channel and remembered my grandmother making these handmade pies from blackberries we picked along the riverbed near her home when I was younger.

    1 lb. fresh black plums or peaches cut into 1/4 inch wedges
    1 egg plus 1 Tbs. water whisked together for egg wash
    1/4 cup sugar
    2 Tbs. orange marmalade or strawberry jam

One 9-inch store bought round pie crust, (1pkg. prepared pie dough (makes 2 pies) Preheat oven to 425'. Remove pie crust from refrigerator 10 minutes before using to soften slightly. Line a baking sheet with parchment. Unfold pie crust onto baking sheet. Spread fig jam on crust leaving a 2-inch border around the edges. Place your plums on top of the jam. Fold the edges over leaving the center exposed and press slightly to seal. Brush outside of the pie dough with egg wash and sprinkle with sugar. Bake until golden, about 45 minutes.

FRESH STRAWBERRIES W/ BALSAMIC SYRUP

1/4 cup brown sugar
1 bunch fresh mint
1½ cups good quality balsamic vinegar
1/4 sugar
2 pints of fresh Strawberries

Here's another way to enjoy the incredible flavors of balsamic reduction with fresh ripe strawberries. Now this is decadent!

Bring the balsamic vinegar and sugar to a boil in a small saucepan over medium heat. Reduce to a simmer and cook, stirring occasionally for about 15 minutes until very thick and syrupy. Set to the side

Wash your strawberries well several times and drain on dish towel. Let them air dry or gently pat them dry with a clean dish towel. Wet strawberries do not dip very well. Arrange strawberries around a dish of brown sugar and another shallow dish of balsamic syrup. Dip strawberries in the sugar or the syrup. Decorate with fresh mint leaves. A nice bubbly Prosecco wine will finish this dessert beautifully. This is a very easy very elegant dessert. Silver Foxes call this the "Kissing" dessert. Oh boy! Try it and you will understand. (You can use many other fruits and small bites in addition to strawberries in this recipe. Use your Silver Fox imagination....

CHOCOLATE SORBET SODA

   1 tall bottle Pellegrino or other sparkling water
   1 pint good quality Chocolate Sorbet or good
      quality ice-cream
   1 bottle of Hershey's Chocolate sauce
   Godiva Chocolate Liqueur *optional
   Fresh mint leaves

Pour a couple tablespoons of chocolate sauce down the sides of a tall slender glass. Add a couple scoops of chocolate sorbet. Fill the glass *slowly* with sparkling water leaving enough room to top with a shot of chocolate liqueur. It will foam up and overflow if you pour the soda in too fast. Serve with a straw and a spoon. Do not forget the straws! You will see what I mean. Eliminate the liqueur if making this for children.

CHOCOLATE GANACHE

This simple chocolate topping goes on anything, just about...

   6 oz. quality dark chocolate bar broken up into pieces
   1 cup heavy cream

Heat the cream in a small sauce pan until almost a boil. Remove pan from the heat and add the chocolate pieces. Stir the mixture until chocolate is completely melted. Use as a decadent dip for fresh fruit or as a glaze over your favorite cake. Store in the refrigerator; heat slowly to use.

FRESH BERRIES & CAKE W/ YOGURT CREAM

3 cups of fresh blackberries, raspberries, blueberries and strawberries (any combination of berries)
1 store bought loaf cake or angel food cake
2 cups of plain thick Greek style yogurt
2 Tbs. Hazelnut flavored coffee creamer
Zest of 1/2 an orange
1 Tbs. powdered sugar
1 Tbs. brown sugar

Wash the berries gently but well, however, be tender with the raspberries as they are very delicate. Drain well on a paper towels then place them in a bowl, and sprinkle with brown sugar. Allow the berries to macerate in their juices while you prepare the yogurt cream. In a medium bowl combine the yogurt, hazelnut flavoring, orange zest, and powdered sugaruntil smooth. Slice the loaf cake into 1 inch thick slices and place 1 slice on each plate. Mound the berries and some of their juices on the slices. Top with a spoonful of the yogurt cream and more berries on top. Fresh, elegant and delicious! Minimum effort here Silver foxes, with maximum rewards!

FRUIT & CHEESE TRAY

This one is so easy... just look at the picture and duplicate what you see. Or make up your own combination with some of your favorites. Select 3 to 5 different cheeses. You can get help at the cheese counter in your super market. Choose fruits that are in season and easily picked up with your fingers like berries, grapes or slices of apple. Include a handful of nuts.

Serve with small crackers.

LEMON PUDDING CAKE

This is a great and easy semi-homemade cake recipe that's been around a long time and still a favorite.

1 cup water
4 eggs
One 18 oz. package lemon cake mix
1 4 oz. package of jello lemon flavor instant pudding and pie filling
1/4 cup oil
1 cup confectioners' sugar
1 Tbs. hot milk
1 tsp. lemon zest

Blend cake ingredients in a large mixer bowl, then beat 2 minutes at medium speed.

Bake in a greased and floured 10-inch Bundt or tube pan at 350 degrees for 55 to 60 minutes, or until cake springs back when lightly pressed. Cool in pan 15 minutes. Turn cake over onto a cake rack to cool completely. Transfer cake to your serving plate.

To make the glaze, gradually add hot milk to lemon zest and confectioners' sugar, blending well. Pour glaze over the top of your cooled cake letting it run down the sides. Yum!

I know some of you silver foxes have never made a cake, but if you want to win hearts, this is worth the effort! Yes, you can do it.

DICK'S 6 PART LIFESTYLE CHANGE PROGRAM

1. FIRST THINGS FIRST! DUMP IT!

The first thing we did was clean out his pantry and the kitchen cabinets, getting rid of all the processed packages of food, the fake sugars and creamers, and junk foods. That just about left nothing on the shelves. Then we did the same to the refrigerator and freezer. There was plenty of outdated jars and bottles of sauce and condiments that had been sitting there way more than a year. Dick had the look of a "deer in the headlights" on his face as I filled several garbage bags with stale, old and some unrecognizable items that had filled his shelves and cabinets. As we made room for the new, we discussed each item and why we were dumping them. He was amazed at what he learned as I pointed out the lists of ingredients and the expiration dates. I don't believe he had ever read a food label in his life up until that day. He began to realize how much sugars, salts, bad fats and chemicals he had been ingesting over the years. Not only that…but how much "fake" food he had been throwing down the old pie hole. Now mind you, he never had to read labels before. He simply let someone else be responsible for what he put in his mouth. But now that he was in charge of the kitchen, and he had to make the decisions, things were going to be different!

2. PLAN AHEAD

"Now what do I do, since there is no food left in the house?" said Dick, looking at me in disbelief and thinly disguised horror at the piles of food on the floor. "First make a list and then grab your checkbook Dick, we're going shopping", I said. "Never ever" I repeated, "ever go to the store without a list, I don't care how short it is". *Always plan ahead.* "I really mean it Dick, only buy what's on your list and that's it"! An hour later, after some careful planning and prioritizing, we headed for the stores.

First stop was Kmart, to purchase a small bullet type blender and a rice cooker. These are relatively inexpensive items that will become invaluable in your kitchen.

Our next stop was the grocery store. Talk about a new experience. Teaching Dick how to navigate the grocery store isles was pretty monumental. The experience really opened his eyes to the myriad of choices both good and bad. I have to agree that serious grocery shopping can be overwhelming for a newbie, especially at the age of 83. But in retrospect, most stores are pretty well laid out and categorized. If you organize your grocery list by separating it into categories, it is so much easier to shop. Group together all the things you will buy in the produce section. You know where I'm talking about; the place where they keep the fruits and vegetables. Do the same with items in the dairy section, meat section, canned foods, Bakery (be careful) etc. Skip the frozen foods section. It has the most temptations and the worst choices. Organizing your list this way will keep you from retracing your steps back and forth through the store. Tracking back and forth up and down the isles' with a heavy cart full of food is not my idea of fun. Or Dicks'! And it's tiring. And your feet start to hurt. Get the picture? Dick sure got it…

3. ORGANIZE IT!

After we finished hauling the groceries and our other purchases into the kitchen, Dick was nearly passing out. He flopped into a chair and looked at me like he wanted to cancel the whole 6 weeks, sure now that he would never survive my plan. His first shopping trip totally took him by surprise. I did assure him that this trip was an exception and it would get easier as he gained confidence in his list, which would hopefully be shorter in the future, and skills navigating the grocery store. We, or more like me, set about the task of dispersing his new healthy groceries into his shelves, cabinets and refrigerator. Dick observed and learned. We created categories for each group of items. For example, fruits and soft vegetables stored together in one bin, onions, garlic, potatoes and the harder vegetables stored together in another bin. Then we stored the dairy items on one shelf, meats and fish on another. Jars, bottles and juices were placed into the doors all neatly organized so when he opened the doors and bins he could see his beautiful healthy food. We filled a large bowl with gorgeous fresh apples, bananas and oranges and set it on the counter within easy reach. After that, I gave Dick a break and cooked a wonderful dinner of baked chicken breast, Quinoa, cooked in his brand new rice cooker, stir fried veggies and a delicious salad of greens, walnuts and sliced tomatoes tossed with red wine vinaigrette. For dessert we ate all the sweet ripe strawberries we could eat. (No sugar, no whipped cream) By then he had regained his composure and was wearing a broad grin. He said it had all been worth it just to eat that great food. Ah, but just wait until tomorrow, I thought as he sat there smiling like the Cheshire cat.

Well, by now you have the idea that getting rid of all the bad stuff, fake food, old and expired bottles and jars, then getting your kitchen organized are the first steps to a better healthy way of eating. Which reminds me... did I mention the cabinets and drawers containing your cooking utensils, pots and pans, kitchen appliances etc. and the rest of the stuff you use to eat off and eat with on a daily basis. Here is where you need to organize some more. Clean out overcrowded cabinets and shelves and move everything including small appliances and your holiday dishes and "stuff" you have not used in the last 6 months to the pantry or convenient storage shelves. Get rid of the "junk"! And what about the products you use to keep your kitchen clean and efficient? Are they eco-friendly? That means they will be friendly to you too.

Ok, so don't give up on me now. I realize it may be painful for some of you to do all this work. But in the long run you will be amazed at how much easier and so much more fun you will have cooking if you know where to find what you need. Really! Dick says "It is true!" and now he knows!

4. MAKING BETTER CHOICES

Ok, so now we talk about making better choices. Each one of us has been inundated with a plethora of information on how to eat better. Using common sense is about all it takes once you have a formula for making a better choice. Don't eat fake food, phony sweeteners and creamers, "diet" stuff, processed foods, low fat, no fat, prepackaged meals and frozen dinners. These we call *Franken Foods.* Stop drinking sodas, sweetened juices and other processed sweet drinks. Make your own iced tea. Eat 3 small meals and up to 2 snacks a day. No more fast foods including all those sweet calorie laden coffee drinks you buy. Yep, I know that is going to hurt some of you. Cut out all trans fats and add healthy fats like olive oil. Do not eat or drink anything with high fructose corn syrup. That's a no, no, no! Eat more fruits and veggies and foods high in natural antioxidants. Be sure to eat all the colorful vegetables. The more colorful the food the higher the antioxidant levels will be. That means "anti-aging benefits" for you. Remember 5 a day? Yes, you can eat more than 5 servings of fruits and vegetables a day, it won't hurt. I promise.

Is there anything left you ask? Well sure there is, and that's where Dick got started and so can you. Start with the labels. Read them. That's why they are on our food. There are many good books on the market that adequately detail how to avoid the bad stuff and make better choices.

Some days Dick and I would go to restaurants for lunch or dinner to discuss the menus and the better and best choices on each. He learned to ask questions of the waiters regarding preparation of his choices, asking for sauces and dressings on the side and less or no added fats like butter and cream, or to request things like steamed vegetables versus sautéed, and grilled and baked versus fried entrées. We talked about *portion size* and the importance of not over eating, especially in the evening. You get the idea. He also added small salads and more vegetables and grains to his meals. I reminded him the more color in a vegetable, the better it is for you. The small changes were easy to make and most restaurants are happy to oblige your reasonable requests. The rice cooker became his new best friend in the kitchen. You can cook several kinds of rice and grains in your cooker. Beautiful fresh ripe fruits were frequently his favorite choice for desserts. And even though he was not "dieting", per say, the change in his diet, the portion size, combined with the walking, stretching and exercises, he began to shed the pounds and feel more energetic and more flexible.

One evening later that week, during our dinner cooking lesson, Dick made a comment about the meal he had just learned to prepare. He said to me "Wow, this food tastes terrific! I have never eaten such wonderful tasting food in my life. I cannot believe how much I am enjoying my food now, and how satisfying it is, and I even know how to cook this now!" And there you have the difference between bags, boxes and cans, and preparing fresh, simple, *REAL* food yourself. Your taste-buds begin to wake up! I do admit you have to take some initiative to do this. But that is what lifestyle change is all about. Get in the kitchen and start cooking! It's worth it!

5. TAKE SOME SUPPLEMENTS

How do I know what supplements to buy for myself? This is a good question. I found a few online websites that are informative and helpful in guiding you to what supplements you need for yourself. Below is a brief summary of information and help you can find at my favorite website www.swansonvitamins.com. I have relied on their website over the years for valuable information and great products. If you are not into the online scene, go to your local Whole Foods or Sprouts Market. They have lots of great informed people to help you make a good decision. Take this guideline with you when shopping for the essential supplements *you* need.

#1 Vitamin & Mineral Complex

A firm foundation for good health depends on vitamins and minerals, which we can get from our diet or from dietary supplements. *Our food is missing many vital nutrients.* Food is different today than it was 100 or even 50 years ago. The Journal of *The American Medical Association* (JAMA), the medical community's most prestigious research journal, announced that all adults should take vitamin supplements to help promote good health.

#2 Calcium and Magnesium

The Recommended Daily Intake (RDI) of calcium is 1000 mg and the RDI of magnesium is 400 mg. From childhood through old age, calcium and magnesium contribute heavily to your health in so many ways. You want to make sure you're getting enough—starting now!

Here are but a few highlights of how calcium & magnesium benefit you:

Noticeably stable and calm moods for all ages—seriously, give it a try!

Strong bones and teeth for a lifetime, *healthy blood pressure*, we overlook this one, but the mineral combo is a *big* factor. *Muscles that work for you, not against you. Deep, uninterrupted sleep—ZZZ!*

#3 Fiber

The National Academy of Sciences recommends 25 grams of fiber per day for women and 38 grams per day for men. Unless you eat lots and lots of fruits and vegetables plus plenty of beans and whole grains, it's hard to get that much fiber from food because the refinement process often removes it.

Fiber supplements like psyllium husks can be your best new friend when it comes to colon health, working like a broom on the walls of the colon to loosen and sweep away all kinds of built up debris. There are different types of fiber like psyllium, pectin, lignans, etc., and each type has its own way of functioning, yet essentially they all work to promote colon health, maintain healthy levels of cholesterol, and support blood sugar health. Start with small amounts of fiber and gradually increase until your stools are the proper consistency and transit time is a consistent 12 to 15 hours.

See Swanson's website for recommendations or speak with someone at your local health food or vitamin store.

#4 Omega 3 Essential Fatty Acids

Fat phobia? Undeniably classed as a fat, EFAs have a tough reputation to overcome in a society where fat is akin to leprosy. If you strictly eschew all fat in your diet, do yourself a favor and work real hard to root out this strongly entrenched notion about it. To be sure, there are fats that you want to avoid like a plague including the hydrogenated fats and trans fatty acids found in fried foods and processed baked goods. These are the kinds of fat that make one fat—and sick! Then there are the essential fatty acids from cold water fish, flaxseeds and walnuts that you should embrace as though they were rare jewels, with Omega-3 EFAs as the most precious of all. What they accomplish in terms of your health truly is priceless! When you visit www.supplementinfo. org, which is the official website of the Dietary Supplement Information Bureau (DSIB), and you view the section "Browse Dietary Supplements," you will find that only vitamins C and E address a greater number of health conditions than Omega-3 Fatty Acids. They even outrank calcium and magnesium! *Brain and Heart Nutrition,* arguably the most important health contributions of Omega-3 EFAs are cognitive function, mood stability, and cardiovascular health. Swanson's has a special section on their website to help you with your EFA selection.

#5 Chlorella

The best food on the planet. Quick, if you could only have one food to eat for the rest of your life, what would it be? While you might be tempted to say cheese burger and fries (that came off my tongue way too fast), you would be oh so smart to revise your answer and choose chlorella, because you truly could live on it a lifetime—a very long lifetime—it's that good for you! Chlorella is perhaps the most nutritionally dense food there is, and many health experts believe that it contains every nutrient required by the human body including vitamins, minerals, amino acids, essential fatty acids, nucleic acids, chlorophyll and a full spectrum of phytochemicals. It bears repeating that most of us aren't choosing particularly healthy foods to provide us nourishment, so chlorella is a great way to pump up the nutritional volume of our meals. It's like getting a hefty serving of fresh, green vegetables.

What does it do? Most noteworthy, chlorella offers super strong support to the immune system, it provides sustained energy that you really notice, and it helps cleanse the body of all kinds of toxins including heavy metals. The list of its capabilities is long and very impressive, and because of its high chlorophyll content, it even neutralizes body odors and bad breath! To learn much more about the health benefits of chlorella, visit www.chlorellafactor.com.

#6 Probiotics

We are what we eat. Many health experts believe that all health issues are related in some way to digestion. This makes sense when you consider the real reason we eat food. While there's no debate that food tastes wonderful, and eating is a fun, social way to spend time with our loved ones, the bottom line is we eat food to live—cold as that sounds. No food, no life! The foods we eat are digested, processed through the intestinal tract, and sent out in a usable form via the blood stream into the cells to provide the necessary material either to repair or replace them. We are wise to do what it takes *now* to maintain good digestion so that our cells are abundantly supplied with what they need, and probiotic supplements can be an extremely effective aid in this endeavor. Probiotics also assist your body's enzymes like protease, amylase and lipase to break down food, insuring greater levels of digestion and absorption.

For this reason, consider a high quality probiotic supplement that provides at least one billion living bacteria per dose, and take it daily as part of your supplement routine for optimal results.

#7 Coenzyme Q10

You've probably heard of Coenzyme Q10, but you may not think of it as a basic supplement like calcium or fiber. Coenzyme Q10 (CoQ10) is a natural, fat-soluble nutrient present in all cells, and it has emerged over the last ten years as the leading supplement for cardiovascular health.

When it comes to keeping your heart healthy and maintaining normal blood pressure levels, many doctors educated about dietary supplements believe CoQ10 is one of the most important nutrients you can take!

The more researchers study it, the more they discover just how crucial it is to neurological health, to the immune system, to blood sugar health, and even to dental health.

CoQ10 has even more to offer. It helps convert food to ATP in the mitochondria of our cells. Like other hormones and enzymes in our body, CoQ10 production peaks in our twenties; then natural levels decline with each passing year. The older we get, the more we notice the good effects of CoQ10 supplementation.

These 7 different supplements are powerful tools to assist you with maintaining your good health for years to come, and if you've been taking these supplements daily as recommended, you are probably feeling pretty super right now. If you are under a Physicians care or take any prescription medications share this list with your Doctor and ask them to recommend the right supplements for you. A good nutritionist can save you a fortune on unnecessary vitamins and useless products, and help you establish guidelines specifically for you. If you would like to know the nutritional values of your food go to *www.freshdirect.org* for detailed information regarding the food you eat. It is amazing what you will learn from this wonderful website. I highly reccomend the following websites for great information on nutrition and supplements.

www.swansonvitamins.com
www.supplementinfo.org
www.freshdirect.org
www.chlorellafactor.com.
www.cookingforsilverfoxes.com.

6. EXERCISE & STRETCHING YOUR BODY

Recommended equipment for these exercises is a yoga mat or beach towel and a good solid chair. That's it!

When you are exercising or stretching remember to use slow movements, especially in the beginning. Starting out too fast will only lead to injury or straining your muscles. Breath slowly and deeply while you are holding your poses. And smile.

CHILD'S POSE

Begin this pose on all fours. Take a slow deep breath and slowly lean back onto your heels, head lowered, arms stretched out in front. This pose opens your spine and relaxes the mind. Sit in this pose for approximately two minutes breathing slowly in and then out. Note: If you feel discomfort in your knees, place a rolled towel behind your knees for support. Close your eyes and visualize your body as strong, healthy and flexible. Keep breathing.

Cat Pose

Pose 1–Back up, head down, butt tucked. Pose 2–Head up, butt up, and back down. On all fours, slowly inhale as you pull the navel towards the spine, pressing the spine towards the ceiling. Slowly exhale pressing the spine towards the floor while rolling the shoulders away from the ears and lifting the head slightly. Take your time. Repeat 10 times and slowly work up to 20 times. Tuck your head down and go into child's pose again and rest for 1 minute.

Leg Pull Ups

Lie on the floor with one knee up. Inhale. Exhale drawing your stomach muscles in while you pull one knee towards your chest. Hold for a count of 10; slowly lower your knee back inhaling slowly as you go. Keep breathing between repetitions. Alternate pulling each knee to your chest and holding for a count of 10. Repeat this ten times.

ONE KNEE PULL UP

TWO KNEES PULL UP

CORE POSE

One of my favorite aspects of stretching is that what seems to be very simple is actually very physically challenging in a quiet way. Always begin with slow deep breathing. For this next exercise just sitting up straight will be challenging for some of you. But give it a try.

Sitting at the end of the chair, sit up as tall as possible and engage the gluts. Pulling the gluts under, hips tilted forward slightly and imagine a string on the top of your head pulling you upwards lifting your head and chest. Close your eyes and imagine you are creating space between each vertebra. Hold this position and deep breathe, in your nose then out your mouth, for 10 to 15 breaths or as long as possible. Repeat five times. You will be surprised what a little oxygen will do for you. You can do this exercise riding in the car, in the office and on an airplane.

CORE POSE WITH A TWIST

Work on your game anywhere! This exercise is not only great for Silver Foxes but incredibly important for the physically challenged golfer. This strengthens your core and increases flexibility. Shave some strokes off your game with this one. Sit back in your chair. Continue from the easy pose as you inhale, lifting the ribcage. Exhale and twist to the left. Utilize your arm over the back of the chair for greater intensity in the pose. Hold for a count of 10. Slowly return to the starting position and repeat five times alternating sides.

SEATED TWISTING POSE

Sitting up as straight as possible with the assistance of your left arm place your left foot on the outside of your right knee. Maintain connection of your left foot to the floor. Place your right arm around your knee. Inhale, lengthening the spine, exhale as you slowly twist to the left and hold to the count of 10. Slowly turn back to your starting position. Repeat five times alternating sides. When Dick started this exercise he leaned on the sofa for stability. He then gradually was able to do it without support. "Hey, you gotta start somewhere" says Dick. So just do it!

Begin all your twisting motions slowly. Your *flexibility will increase* over time. I know; it's hard to believe. Dick couldn't imagine it either. But with lots of laughing and groaning he did it! Even after years of a sedentary lifestyle, it made a difference for Dick. It made a difference in his stride. What difference could it make for you?

The next step for Dick was to get moving again. Strengthening your core muscles is key for this next activity. Walking gets oxygen into your lungs and blood, gets your cardio up, increases your circulation, and strengthens your legs and butt, which hold up the rest of you and keep you moving through life. Pretty important stuff!

7. GET MOVING!

WALKING IS YOUR FRIEND

Well, the second day, bright and early, I presented Dick with a floppy hat to keep the sun off his nose and a bottle of water. The blank look in his eyes told me he had no idea what he was in for. After a little stretching and our morning drink, we headed out the front door. "Nope, Dick said", he could not even taste the eggs in his shake.

The first day we walked a few steps, stopped, walked a few more steps, groaned a lot, stopped, walked a few more steps, stopped again, whined some, drank some water, walked another step or two…you get the picture. It was not pretty! Ok, so we did laugh too, at first. Believe me, I know this is not easy when you've had health issues or are not used to walking. The idea here is not to set any records, just get moving! Put one foot in front of the other. Get out of the chair and start adding steps each day. Dick went from couch potato to road warrior in six weeks. His body began to change and so did his social life.

Why is walking important you say? I just can't get out of the chair, I hurt all over, I'm too tired… blah blah blah. Ok, it's simple dear ones… including you Dick, you either move it or you lose it! And once you are walking on a regular basis you will find that you feel so much better and walking will energize you instead of wearing you out. All that oxygen in your lungs and sunshine on your face will make you look soooo good!

HOW TO GET STARTED

Get out the door and *walk* 4 to 5 times a week. *Start out slow*, walking for just 5 to 10 minutes a day without stopping. This is not a race, just keep moving. Add 5 minutes every 3 days until you are able to *walk* for at least 30 minutes or more. Stop and rest as needed, but try to keep moving. Use a little journal or personal calendar and check off the days you walk and for how long. Dick was walking for 30 to 45 minutes 4 to 5 times a week. He even got to where he was able to walk a mile in 36 minutes which was awesome progress for such a couch potato.

Ok, so some of you road warriors say you are already walking. Good for you. This means you are at the head of the pack! Show 'em how it's done! Start a walking club in the neighborhood. Get your friends and relatives off the couch and help each other reach your walking goals. I believe in you!

Eat something before you plan to walk. A good breakfast shake or a banana first thing in the morning will give you the energy to get your walk done. If you walk later in the day, a good snack before you walk is a great idea.

Stretch! Doing a full stretching program such as was illustrated earlier, is the best way to start the day and your walking program. Stretching the legs and calves is *always* recommended before walking.

Hydrate – Always hydrate before and during your walks. Drink a big glass of water before going out the door and be sure to take a full water bottle with you. Stop about every 10 minutes, or as often as you like, for a good chug of water. But keep moving. You can do it!

There are many different kinds of inexpensive *water bottles* and packs available at your local stores like Target, Walmart and Sports Authority.

What to wear—Wear *weather appropriate clothing* and *good walking shoes*. You can get help finding the right shoes for you at your local athletic shoe stores. Layers of clothing can be removed or added for your comfort. Wear a hat, yep, just get any old hat. Cover your head from the sun.

What to take—Do take your cell phone in case you need a ride home, or in case of emergency. Take a *full water bottle* and *lip balm*. Carry a *food bar* tucked in your pocket, or a piece of fruit in case you need something to eat. Don't forget to wear your *sunglasses*. They make you look so cool out there on the street, but really; they're good for your eyes.

To *add dimension to the walking experience* we played kick the can as we walked. This activity worked some new leg muscles Dick forgot he had. It also helps to regain some balance when you alternate kicking with both legs. If you have access to a treadmill and cannot get out the door, follow the same approach as walking, except don't try kicking the can on the treadmill. Get a stuffed animal and kick it around the house. You will be surprised how therapeutic it is.

We also picked up fist size stones and "pumped iron" as we walked to add to our workout. Weight bearing exercises are good for your bones and core strength. You can carry small weights as you walk. You can adapt these ideas to your own neighborhood.

The most wonderful part of our walks for Dick was getting out of the house. The serendipity… there were real people out there. We made friends with everyone we met as we walked and kicked and pumped our way through the neighborhood. It was great fun greeting the same walkers each day. A former lead trumpet player, Dick was used to playing to a crowd and you can be sure he bestowed his charm on everyone we met. This is where *his new social life began to take shape*. He began to receive invitations for dinner from his new friends and Dick even threw a couple dinner parties and invited the neighbors back. He had a ball shopping and cooking dinner for his guests. In the process Dick became more comfortable shopping and especially finding new interest in the kitchen. He began to see eating as more than just stuffing the old pie hole with whatever was in front of him. Food and eating began to take on a whole new meaning for Dick.

…Fast forward to June, 2012. It's dinner time at Dick's house.

The old jazz standards play in the background. Candles flicker across the room. Friends and family take their seats around the long wooden dinner table in anticipation of the coming meal. Wonderful aromas waft through the air. Corks are pulled and wine poured. Dick sits at the head of the table watching as plates of food are passed. His eyes light up and a big smile spreads across his face. He surveys his "audience", seemingly setting up his marks, and once again he steps on stage…Diving into his plate of food, Dick laughs heartily and begins charming the women, and wisecracking with the men. His wife Lolita looks up at Dick and smiles. With a big grin on his face Dick smiles back and says "How can you ask for more than that"?

There are no guarantees that Dick will live a longer life as a result of his transformation. But Dick doesn't care. He lives a fuller, happier, more satisfying life now that he takes responsibility for his health and well- being. Not only that, he feels great. And since his lovely wife Lolita has recovered from an injury and returned home, he loves to get dressed up and take her out for lunch or dinner now and then.

ABOUT DICK

Darko (Dick) Kolar emigrated to the U.S. with his maternal grandmother as a young 3 yr. old child from Yugoslavia some 82 years ago. Later, his mother joined them. He grew up in the Chicago area in the 1930's and 40's. By the time he was in high school he was blowing a trumpet and swinging with the likes of Lee Konitz, Sonny Stitt, and Gene Ammons in the Harold Fox band. At the age of 23 Dick was leading his own 16 piece orchestra in the style of Count Basie and Duke Ellington, called the "Dick Kolar Orchestra". He played many of the big dance ballrooms in the jazz district of Chicago in the 50's and early 60's. During the 60's and 70's Dick bred and raised champion quarter horses on his ranch in Colorado. He is known for his world champion quarter horse named "Mercedes Impressive".

Later, for health reasons, he moved to the California coast then finally settled in Arizona where he built another career as a successful real estate developer. All the while his roots in the jazz world influenced everything he touched and everyone he met.

ABOUT THE AUTHOR

My love for cooking and great food began at an early age. Both my grandmothers were wonderful cooks; one, a city girl whose roots were proper English and German, the other a German farm girl whose shed was always bursting with homemade preserves, pickles and dried herbs hanging from hooks on the ceiling.

During the 70's I traveled through Europe and lived a short time in the Middle East. Shopping the bazaars and open air markets for exotic foods and spices was a heady experience for me. I searched for new and unusual recipes everywhere I went.

Growing up in southern California I embraced the "healthy lifestyle." During the 80's, as the co-owner of 3 restaurants, I spent many hours in the kitchen with the chefs learning to make stocks and sauces, Quiche Lorraine and Eggs Oscar. I helped develop the menu and the dishes we served. It was then I began my own organic kitchen garden.

After moving to Arizona at the end of 1989 I found it next to impossible to grow anything in the caliche filled desert soil. Determined to find a way to have my garden again I enrolled in Arizona State University classes and became a "Master Gardener of the Low Desert". Eventually my raised bed gardens were published in Sunset Magazine. I happily won many ribbons for my herbs and jams and prize winning plants at the Arizona State Fair.

In 1991 I earned the distinction of C.T. from the International Academy of Clinical Acupuncture and traveled through China with a group of doctors to observe and learn from Traditional Chinese Medicine practitioners. It was a trip of a lifetime. Not to mention the new and exotic foods I experienced along the way.

In 2008 I graduated as a Health Coach and began combining all the valuable skills I learned over the years to help people change their "Lifestyle" to a healthier, more joyous and satisfying one.

Great passion for cooking led me to share my abilities with friends and others. Hence I began to write about some of these food exploits and my book "Cooking for Silver Foxes and other First Time Cooks" was born.

To me, life, love and great food are inseparable. I have five wonderful children who also love to cook and five incredible grandchildren continually reminding me how grand I am.

Ashling Clair Reve

Lifestyle Health Coach, Author, Personal Chef, Master Gardener, Artist and Entrepreneur

INDEX